M000317007

A RACE AGAINST
TIME

**BRITISH
NORTH
GEOMAGNETIC
POLE
EXPEDITION
1 9 9 2**

A RACE AGAINST TIME

TIME
BRITISH
NORTH
GEOMAGNETIC
POLE
EXPEDITION
1992

DAVID HEMPLEMAN - ADAMS

Published in 1993 by
The Self Publishing Association Ltd
Units 7/10, Hanley Workshops,
Hanley Road, Hanley Swan,
Worcs.

in conjunction with
DAVID HEMPLEMAN-ADAMS

British Library Cataloguing in Publication Data

A catalogue record for this book is available from the British Library

ISBN 1 85421 199 4

Designed and Produced by Images Design and Print Ltd
Printed and bound in Great Britain by Hartnolls Ltd, Bodmin, Cornwall

CONTENTS

DEDICATION

To Claire and Alicia

AUTHOR'S NOTE

There are numerous reasons for writing books related to exploration and adventure. Some authors write for money, some to provide advice and guidance to those aspiring to similar adventures; others wish to write an informative report on a specific event. My own reasons are a concoction of all three.

My introduction to adventure began with my participation in the Duke of Edinburgh Awards Scheme, and was further developed through the encouragement of Mansell James, Roy Knight and John Price, old school masters who taught and slowly involved me in adventurous activities. From this initial encouragement the die was cast.

When preparing for my Arctic expeditions I am always aware of the considerable information and guidance that has been made available to me through the writings of other explorers, people like Fiennes, Shackleton and Herbert, all of whom gave an insight into these beautiful areas.

It is my hope that this book will inspire others to meet a challenge. That it will underline both the frustration and importance of careful planning, the hardships which must be endured, and, eventually, the incredible satisfaction of success.

But primarily, the book provides me with an opportunity to thank everyone who helped with the expedition.

Obviously, the members of the team are high on the list. From day one it was their fortitude and ability to overcome considerable difficulties which ensured success.

As a team we were supported by a great number of people who entered enthusiastically into the many chores involved in preparing the expedition. In particular, everyone at Robnor, especially Lynne, Jackie, Margaret, Sue and Tina, who wrote thousands of letters.

My thanks go to all our sponsors, so generous with time and help, especially Keith Rugg of Burton McCall and John Nelligan of Brittania

Music Club. Thanks also to Jill Parry, a constant source of help and encouragement, and Norman Smith for assisting in putting this book together.

My lasting thanks to the May family and the Advantek organisation. Jim May, who established Advantek was the expedition's major sponsor.

Jim and my father have been firm friends for twenty years. Once committed, Jim came to England to help and encourage, and later came up to Resolute to undertake the final act of any sponsor; to pick us all up safely from the ice at our ultimate goal. I will never forget Jim's son Jeff May yomping over the ice from the pick up 'plane to meet us with a six-pack of beer. What an awesome sight!

Jim's daughter Elaine came up to Resolute accompanied by Shirley Chenoweth to operate the radios and were there for the duration of the expedition. Radio contact with Elaine was the highlight at the end of an exhausting day and she was aptly named Resolute Rose.

Later she came to England to help me prepare the script for the book, a task which had to be completed in a short space of time and involved pounding a Word Processor into the early hours.

I would like to thank all my family and friends, too numerous to mention, who have helped and supported me over the years. Without them and the significant support of Jim May, the expedition and consequently this book, would not have been possible.

Last but not least, I must thank Claire and Alicia who have put up with my antics for so long.

I love them very much. When you are cold, hungry and desperate, you come to realise just how much your family means to you.

All the profits from this book will go into a Trust Fund which contributes towards providing opportunities for children to gain experience of the wilderness and adventure on annual camps.

PART ONE

THE BEGINNING 1980 - 1992

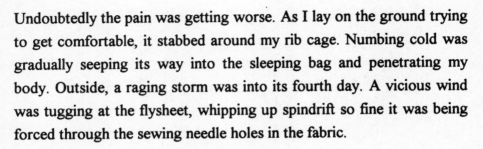

CHAPTER ONE

A DIAMOND IN THE COALFIELD

Undoubtedly the pain was getting worse. As I lay on the ground trying to get comfortable, it stabbed around my rib cage. Numbing cold was gradually seeping its way into the sleeping bag and penetrating my body. Outside, a raging storm was into its fourth day. A vicious wind was tugging at the flysheet, whipping up spindrift so fine it was being forced through the sewing needle holes in the fabric.

"God, please get me out of this!"

What a mess, would I ever get home? Trapped in a tent, I was tired, hungry and frightened; hundreds of miles from anywhere and waiting for a rescue flight, acutely aware each hour that passed that the pack ice was moving further away from the pick-up location given to the base.

I was attempting to get to the Geographical North Pole solo, without the use of dogs or snowmobiles. Many people had said it was fool-hardy and impossible. It was beginning to occur to me that they might have had a point. Should I try and walk back? The temptation to follow this course of action was psychologically strong. I wanted to be "up and doing". However, logic convinced me that it would mean certain death in this storm. Patience was the only answer.

I had a number of hours in which to think. Obviously, this was the end of the expedition. In retrospect, it was apparent my lack of experience had left me ill-prepared. My equipment had not been adequate, neither had I been physically or mentally ready to cope with these extreme conditions. However, the trip had given me an insight to the necessary techniques for survival in this harsh environment. I swore I would return to make another attempt.

Opening my diary and retrieving a pencil from the depths of the sleeping bag, I passed the time by jotting down a few notes under various headings. "Sledge – needs to be bigger, with a canopy. Easier ties, etc, etc." Under each heading – skis, food, tent, clothing, stove, sleeping bag – ran several lines of comments for future consideration. For Team (why had I subconsciously put "team" instead of "solo"?), I pencilled in the name Steve Vincent and gradually added others. Following this, I put "experience and training"; I had certainly learnt my lesson the hard way, for I added, "Where on earth do you get experience of this hell hole other than by being here?"

Another day passed, and, to my surprise, the wind stopped as quickly as it started. Through the open door of the tent, beautiful blue skies were revealed. I radioed to base – "Weather positive, weather positive."

Georgio "Mac" Matranga's voice boomed back, "OK, old man, will try a rescue from Caesar. Talk to you in one hour."

Caesar was a floating ice scientific station just thirty minutes' flying time from my present position. Eventually, the radio crackled into life once more. "Kim*, Kim, a 'plane should be over you ETA any moment. How do you read?"

As I made the reply "Roger-Roger", the hum of an aircraft began to signal its approach and with some satisfaction I heard it getting closer and closer.

_____

* Kim is my middle name used by close friends

17

I crawled out of the tent, hardly believing my eyes. It was an emotional moment. Pain made it difficult to stand upright, tears had started to well up and there was a lump in my throat. I was going to survive.

Putting down on to the snow, the Twin Otter bumped and yawed its way over to me. The pilot jumped out. Walking over to me, he shook my hand and said, "Congratulations."

"What for?" I asked. As far as I was concerned, I had failed miserably.

"Well, you walked two hundred and thirty miles and spent forty-two days out here and lived, that's success."

His philosophy fell on deaf ears. Now, in the relatively balmy position of safety, I was becoming increasingly angry with myself and at the mistakes I had made. "I'll be back, don't you worry."

A man of few words, the Pilot said, "Why don't you shut up and relax. Get into the 'plane while we pack your kit up."

This sounded good advice to me.

Once back in Resolute, a reporter 'phoned and asked, "What's it like to be a failure?" It occurred to me that any reporter having to resort to this level of questioning might not be unfamiliar with failure himself. However, looking at a photograph of Claire, I answered, "It's nice just to be a live failure."

At the hospital, the Medics diagnosed two cracked ribs, the result of falling from the top of a pressure ridge during the walk. Steve Vincent chuckled at my being bandaged up. "No pain, no gain," he smirked. It's amazing the way the suffering of a friend brings out the humour in us.

"You wait, you'll see what it's like," I told him. We headed for home.

It was strange to be flying South once again, back to civilisation. Like coming from the stone age back to the glaring twentieth century. It felt such an anti-climax, after all that planning and hustling to get equipment and sponsorship.

Our bedraggled team walked into Montreal Airport for the flight home. Nobody likes a loser, and this was perfectly illustrated by Canadian Pacific Airlines. They were extremely generous in giving myself and the support team first class tickets all the way to Canada, but, because I had failed, we were all going home economy class.

In typical fashion, the armchair experts at home said it had been silly to try the impossible. No doubt the man who invented the wheel had received the same encouragement! Nevertheless, I asked myself, was it a foolhardy enterprise? What had made me attempt it?

Mountaineering, my first love, was going through a radical change. Rock climbers were now climbing with a bag of chalk and nothing else in the way of equipment, and far outstretching routes hitherto undreamed of in climbing circles. Even on the big mountains, in the Alps and Himalayas, routes were being climbed in true Alpine style. Expeditions were becoming smaller, yet bolder. Messner really epitomised the purist form of climbing: small expeditions, often solo and without oxygen, culminating in his classic solo climb of Everest. Arctic expeditions, on the other hand, were still slogging away with huge expensive teams, mountains of equipment, dog teams and snowmobiles.

If I had succeeded on the Geographical Pole, my intention was to try the next step up the rungs of the ladder: a solo expedition to the

Magnetic Pole, without the use of dogs and snowmobiles, but also without that valuable help, the aeroplane – the purest form of travel. Could it be done? And which objective to try first: the Magnetic or the Geographical Pole again?

Given the right equipment, I felt that the Geographical was a possibility. The Magnetic would be a shorter distance, and easier ice, but the paulk would be much heavier, and, psychologically, it would be a test of strength as I wouldn't have those important visits with food and "goodies".

On my return I went to Radstock near Bath, to see my old PE Master, Mr Mansell James. Affectionately known as "Jesse" to the lads, he had been a surrogate father to me at school. It was his guidance and encouragement which led me into adventure through the Duke of Edinburgh's award.

Over a couple of cans of lager I went through my thoughts with him. Finally he said, "Well, boyo, the Geographical Pole seems like an easier trip, why don't you do that?"

Jesse knew me too well. I immediately said, "Right, the Magnetic Pole it is then."

At which he smiled back, "I thought you'd say that." I had fallen for it hook, line and sinker.

There was less than eight months to organise the Magnetic Pole Expedition, due to the problems of melting ice in the Summer-time. The first priority was to organise the support team. Steve Vincent was newly married and couldn't go. Mac's Mum wouldn't let him go again. However, luck had not deserted me. At the BBC bar I met Steve

Morris, who had been the cameraman on the Geographical Pole Trip, and I posed the question, "How about another cold holiday?" Steve is tremendously likeable and incredibly professional at his job. He agreed, after being plied with four more pints. He was a marvellous catch.

John Burgess was approached whilst engaged in making modifications to my sledge. A man with true Yorkshire grit, he is first class at improvisation. He instantly jumped at the chance of going to the Arctic.

I wanted to make the expedition a low-key effort, just in case I failed again. There seemed to be little point in massive media coverage just to promote a failure. Nevertheless, I had an obligation to my sponsors, who supported me with cash and equipment. A compromise was finally reached. I managed to persuade Nick Schoon, a local reporter on the *Western Daily Press*. If I succeeded, in order to keep the sponsors happy, we would relay the news and capitalise on the result. I took an instant liking to Nick. In all my dealings with the media, he was one individual who was absolutely professional whilst demonstrating the highest level of integrity. A genuinely nice man.

Over the remaining time left to us each piece of equipment was checked and rechecked, and a hundred modifications were made to eliminate, as far as possible, the chance of a malfunction.

The team – Steve Morris, John Burgess, Nick Schoon – and myself met up at Stansted Airport in April 1984. Not the nightmare of the year before. With a support team consisting of just three members, we had less than two hundred and fifty pounds of equipment to load aboard the aircraft, compared with two thousand pounds the previous year. Feeling mildly confident, I felt so much easier and relaxed without the media watching in case one of us managed to make some "newsworthy" mistake.

Canadian Pacific sponsored us again with economy flights up to Resolute Bay, North-West Canada. Time flew in a whirl of activity. Toronto, Montreal, Frobisher, then arrival at Resolute to see familiar faces again. I was planning to leave by the back door on Monday and head for the Pole.

The previous year it had taken nearly two months to set up base and reach the same stage of readiness. Experience had taught us all a great deal. We tested the Bradley's Radio, fired the rifle, checked the Argos satellite navigation system, which would give irrefutable documentation of reaching the Pole. Tent, stoves, sleeping bags, sledge, all had been modified and tested from the last expedition. Even the food was changed. I couldn't eat another bowl of porridge if it was the last food in the world. My intention was to have a nutritious diet, but one which I also enjoyed. None of this pemmican and butter for me. Pre-cooked Goulash, stew and casserole would be the order of the day.

It was time for my departure. Steve Morris had persuaded a young Mountie to dress in his official attire to see me off. It was incongruous to see me kitted out for -60°C whilst he shivered clad only in his red uniform, jumping in and out of his truck to avoid frostbite.

Then away. Straight down the rough beach outside of Bradley's (the Aircraft Support Company), heading for the frozen sea. I could feel the sledge was much heavier than before, approximately two hundred pounds. Each step jolted me to a standstill, until I got onto the flat ice. Even then, it was hard going.

The first night's camp was still in sight of Resolute. The radio sked[*] blasted into the tent. The voices of Steve and John were so loud it seemed as if you could reach out and touch them.

Everything went smoothly until day six. I reached Stanley Head, the jumping off point from Cornwallis Island to Little Cornwallis Island. Observing tell tale signs of fast-moving cloud gathering, and from the weather forecast I had received, I knew I was in for a real hooley and didn't fancy wasting valuable food and fuel with a "wait-out" so soon into the trip. However, that evening it blew a full gale. I battened down the hatches, and felt reasonably secure. Older and wiser, I now had the patience and experience to wait it out.

My composure was shattered when I heard a noise outside, then a distinct sound of sniffing. I knew immediately what it was. Instinctively I started to scream as the head of a polar bear came in through the side of the tent. Grabbing the rifle and still yelling, I cocked the gun and fired it into the ground. This could not have taken more than a few seconds, but it seemed more like ten minutes to me. The shot scared the bear away. A few moments later I tentatively opened the tent zip and saw the bear about twenty-five yards away looking at me. A bitter wind was biting at the tent and me, but the bear was oblivious to it all. It started coming towards me. I tried another warning shot at its side, to no avail. The bear started to charge. Beyond doubt, this was a determined attack.

I had been advised, that should I meet this situation, the practice was to kneel down, breathe slowly and exhale whilst squeezing the trigger, on no account pulling it, and to be sure to aim at the bear's body, as the bullet might ricochet off its skull.

––––––––––––––––––––––––

[*] A scheduled radio call.

So much for the practice. In the real situation, my rifle was shaking so much that "aim" was converted to "spray". Whilst he kept coming, I kept firing. I pumped the brute so full of lead he would have drowned, he had so many holes in him. Eventually, the bear dropped twelve feet from my tent. I quickly reloaded and went to where it lay, shouting and screaming, "You silly bastard, why did you make me kill you?" I was super-charged with adrenaline which had made me oblivious of the fact that I was in danger of freezing to death. The attack had left me with no time to get my cold weather gear on. I pulled back into the tent and quickly tried to revive my frozen hands and feet.

It was conditional for travelling in the High Arctic that, should you shoot a polar bear, the wildlife authorities would want the carcass picked up and would also want a damn good reason for shooting it. Polar bears are not an endangered species, however, you simply cannot go around shooting them. Each village has a quota, and this bear came off the Resolute tag quota.

It took an hour before I could radio Steve and John. I was still shaken. I couldn't contact them because of a radio black-out, so I put the emergency switch on the Argos. An hour later I had calmed down and stopped shaking. I then realised, although I had put the emergency button on, it wasn't a real emergency. I stepped down the signal to the next message. "Pick up requested A.S.A.P."

An hour later, a Twin Otter was overhead. Bruce Jonasson, the Bradley's manager jumped out of the 'plane. Eyeing up the situation he said, "Christ! That was close."

The incident had its amusing side, which developed whilst we attempted to get a fully grown male bear weighing about four hundred pounds into the aircraft. Each of us took a leg but that was no good.

Two men tried to get under it in an attempt to lift it. Various other ingenious methods were tried and failed. It turned into farce that would not have disgraced a John Cleese sketch. The bear's contribution was to make liberal post mortis bowel movements. At last, with the 'plane loaded, Bruce took the bear back to Resolute, leaving me once again lonely on the cold ice.

The expedition that was supposed to be kept from the world's press was suddenly world news. I really was in the dog house for killing this lovely little teddy bear. The fact that I had been its intended breakfast, was not a point to be discussed. "Man Kills Bear" – that's news, "Bear Kills Man" – now that really is news!

I headed for the Polaris Mine, and camped down in the bay. Steve and John flew to the mine, came down to meet me, and were silent when I told them about the bear incident. It made me even more paranoid, as I was now to head up to Bathurst Island, across an area called Polar Bear Pass, reputedly so-named because of the high concentration of bears. Each night I slept with the zip undone on my sleeping bag and tent, and placed my sledge thirty yards from the tent with food on the top, the theory being a bear might be partial to Mars Bars in preference to man meat, disturb the sledge, wake me up, and give me valuable seconds to respond. I hoped the theory worked.

Gradually I made my way up the coast until one day I came across some sticky brown ice. I nicknamed this place the Venus Fly Trap. Continuing to progress North, I was drawn increasingly into this mushy zone. Realising this might be leading to open water, I decided to make a large detour over to the coast. About three hundred yards from land, my right leg and ski suddenly went through the ice. My heart was in my mouth. Praying to all the gods of the world to help me out, gingerly, I managed to crawl away from the broken crust.

Kneeling down, and shaking uncontrollably, I started to heave with fright. I prayed, shook and heaved until reaching solid land. Erecting the tent, putting the radio dipoles out, I called up Bradley's. Steve came over loud and clear. He was surprised at the call, as it was off the usual radio sked time. Going through the drama with him, I told him I wanted to be picked up. That if I had gone through completely with my sledge, I would have gone down like a torpedo. My bottle had gone, I wanted to go home.

"Just wait an hour," he advised, "get some food and drink into you." He told me they would radio again in one hour to discuss whether or not I should give up.

An hour went by, and the next sked. "I want to go home." No going back, I didn't like this game anymore.

Steve was very calm and concise. "Look, no problem about picking you up. Just have some more tea and we'll have another sked in an hour."

I was a little surprised an hour later when John Burgess came on to the radio.

"I hear you want to give up."

"That's right, when can you get to me?"

A Yorkshire tirade came through the air. "If you think you are going to get me and Steve up here and return home, trip unfinished, because some sissy doesn't like water, you've got another think coming. You get walking in the morning and get on with it."

I was so shocked I said, "Right then, if you feel like that, I'll show you." He had saved the expedition.

26

Although the sledge was gradually becoming lighter, the remainder of the trek was not without incident. Physical effort was beginning to take its toll, making me feel run-down and tired. I began to suffer from bleeding piles making every step agony and I had to walk with a sanitary towel stuffed between my cheeks.

A frustrating situation awaited me when I got onto the open pack ice. My aim, as I said, was to get to the Magnetic Pole, having been given its position by the Geological Survey. In theory, the Pole will dip at 90°, but in practice it moves hourly, in an oval, clockwise configuration. There was a possibility I could actually pull through its outer ring and head for the centre of the ring. Unfortunately, I could only navigate by using a sun compass, the standard magnetic compasses being useless. I had a nautical almanac and could use the sun's shadow to determine the direction I'd need to go. There is a snag with this system. No sun, you're stuck.

One day, in total white-out, I was getting very close to the Pole and feeling tremendously excited. It was essential to keep making distance. I tried the sun shadow – nothing! I then thought of a wheeze. If I did a 360° rotation with the light meter in my camera, the direction where the biggest deflection occurred should in theory be the brightest spot, and consequently the sun. I was chuffed that I had worked this out. If you knew where the sun was, you could create your own shadow and walk in the right direction.

I did this for five hours, each hour changing the shadow to comply with the almanac. Suddenly I came across some tracks. I felt like Robinson Crusoe seeing human tracks for the first time in weeks. I didn't know of another expedition in this area. I sat on Sibyl – my sledge – and chewed on some Mars Bar chunks. Then it dawned on me. I had walked in a full circle.

I erected the tent and put the Argos on, radioed Steve and told them the story. They all advised staying put until I could see the sun clearly. I was so dejected. Only twenty miles to go, so close.

By 8.00 that night the sun poked its head out of the clouds. I was instantly heartened and excited. The sledge now weighed only about forty pounds. I decided to do four hours blitz and then camp again. This was the season when the sun can be clearly visible twenty-four hours a day. However, there is still a distinct day and night temperature.

Starting off at 8.00 p.m. it was colder, but it was good to get going and make up for lost time. There was no sign of land to be seen anywhere. I expected to see the mountains to the North, but there was nothing in sight. Anxious to maintain progress, I shot off, panting and blowing like an old cart horse. Midnight came, up went the tent, into the maggot – sleeping bag – down with the pre-packed flask of chocolate and to sleep. Maybe just one more day to go.

Once again the alarm shook me from the depths of my dreams. It was fortunate that I had decided on the sprint the night before, or I would have been awake all night with nervous excitement.

At 7.00 a.m. the radio crackled into life. Steve gave me the updated Argos position. I was tremendously relieved to hear I had made excellent progress, most importantly in the right direction. A good day would do it.

Steve told me to keep the Argos on and radio in every two hours to get my position. There was now less than twelve miles to go. Was this the time to ditch all the extra weight and make the going easier? It was tempting, but the experience of the storms the previous year had made me cautious. "Don't gash anything until the 'plane lands." Away I went at a sprint. Stop on the hour, drink, eat, away again. On the second hour, I quickly rigged the radio. How far had I gone? They said they didn't know. It took at least an hour to process the reading. Just keep going.

After two more hours, I put the dipoles up again. "How far have I gone?"

"Two miles."

"Two miles? Never."

"Just keep going, faster."

By now, I was well aware what pace I was doing, and was sure I was making a good three miles a hour. At that speed four hours should have given me the Pole.

"How could I only have gone two miles?" It should have been twelve, I was starting to get worried.

Go, go, go, you lazy cuss! It was all or nothing. Another six hours. Dipoles up. "How far have I gone now?"

"Four miles."

What were they playing at? I must have done eighteen miles. Maybe I wasn't going as fast as I thought, maybe I was going in the wrong direction. Steve said to carry on for another two hours.

I was exhausted. I didn't pace myself, progress reduced to two miles an hour. Dipoles up after eight hours.

"Steve, seriously, what have I done?"

"Just another three miles to go."

"How can that be? Eight hours and only nine miles?" I worked out I must have done twenty-one miles. Well over the Pole. What on earth was going on?

Steve said they were leaving right away to pick me up, so I

decided to keep walking until they found me, to make up the last three miles. I kept the Argos on. It suddenly dawned on me, I might be going home tonight. It gave me the added incentive to carry on, but I could now hardly pull my sledge. Each step, the rope over my shoulder pulled tight on my shattered body.

I placed the Saabi beacon and flares on the top of the sledge. After two hours I stopped. No more, this was killing me. I put the tent up and threw the maggot inside. I was beyond caring whether they picked me up or not.

The moment I started to crawl into the tent I heard the Otter. I tripped trying to get the Saabi, fumbling away with the flares. One off, two off. The Otter with its landing lights on came diving down and waggled its wings. Jim Merritt, who did most of my resupplies in the previous year's expedition, and to my mind was the finest Arctic Pilot in the world, jumped down. A slow Canadian drawl, "Well done, what took you so long?" Steve, John and Jack Napper (our expedition sponsor) all followed Jim out of the Otter and started to pat me on the back.

Steve said, "Why did you walk ten miles further than you needed to?" I couldn't believe it! He had conned me into walking through and over the Pole.

At last, the sweet taste of success. The champagne and tears flowed in equal amounts.

Over the dressing room door leading out to Centre Court at Wimbledon is the following quotation by Rudyard Kipling: "If you can meet with triumph and disaster and treat those two impostors just the same . . . " I knew which impostor I enjoyed.

We flew back to Resolute, and then straight back to Montreal.

We had the flip coin of sponsorship on the way home. We had flown out economy. Having succeeded, we were all flying home first class. A fickle world. The flight back was a moment for thoughts of contentment. Another piece had been added to the jigsaw of my experience.

On returning to the UK I gave a series of lectures on the Geographical and Magnetic Poles. During the previous year I lectured at Ludgrove Preparatory School and had been invited back. Later it was to become Prince William's prep school. At the conclusion of a lecture, I was always staggered by the foresight of some of the questions youngsters would come up with. How long can you live without water, food? How cold is -40°C to -60°C? Why don't polar bears freeze? Very much to the point, I just dreaded the questions afterwards.

After the lecture at Ludgrove Prep, a young lad came up and asked, "What's the difference between the Magnetic Pole and the Geomagnetic Pole?"

I thought for a moment, and then said it was the same.

"Oh no it's not," he chanted, "there is a difference."

"How do you know?" I asked, getting ready to give him a thick ear.

"Because it's at the back of the Times Atlas."

At that he ran off.

Two minutes later, we were all huddled over this huge book. "There you are," he shouted with triumph.

I came clean, I didn't know the difference. It also seemed there was a corresponding Pole in the Antarctic. But the Geomagnetic Pole was distinctly marked just off the West coast of Greenland, in the

31

Kane Basin. A stretch of water separated Ellesmere Island in Canada from Greenland.

Ironically, I felt I knew the area well. The first book I had ever read on the subject of Arctic Exploration, written by Lord Edward Shackleton, Earnest Shackleton's son, was about the Oxford University Ellesmere Island Expedition. It was reading this book at the age of eleven that first got me interested in the polar regions.

On returning home that night, I immediately re-read the book. Then I re-read Wally Herbert's *Across the Top of the World*. Herbert had spent much time in this area. Neither he nor Shackleton mentioned the Geomagnetic Pole. I had never heard of any expedition reaching this point, and in fact, except for the young schoolboy, I had never even heard anyone talking about it.

I had flown around and visited this area with the RAF, staying at Thule Airforce Base. Again, no one had ever mentioned it. I contacted the Geological Survey, Royal Geographical Society and Scott Polar Society. There was indeed a Geomagnetic North Pole! Its position had moved into the middle of the Kane basin, and as far as all the researchers could find out, no one had ever been there.

An inquisitive young boy had given me a diamond in a coal field.

(top) Shot polar bear on Magnetic Pole Expedition.
(above) Thin ice - I got a cold dip once before.

RCMP bidding farewell from Resolute - start of Magnetic
Pole Expedition 1984.

Slumped with cracked ribs - the failed Geographical Pole Expedition 1983.

Beautiful surroundings - solo Magnetic Pole.

Success at last - Magnetic Pole

Face iced up.

CHAPTER TWO

THE FIRE FROM WITHIN

The more research I did into the Geomagnetic Pole, the more interested I became. It appeared that two options presented themselves for consideration. The first of these would be to start the expedition from Thule in Greenland, taking the much shorter route up the coast of Greenland and into the Kane Basin. This would be similar to the route taken by the Innuit hunters and Shackleton on his sledge journeys. It was tempting, but could present problems when dealing with the Danish authorities who are keen on insurance bonds and back-up, to a point which can become excessive. The other alternative was to go from Grise Fjord or Eureka. Starting from Eureka would mean crossing Ellesmere Island, a route which would give the added bonus of beautiful scenery.

At this stage, I was fully intending to make it a solo expedition, so I read Wally Herbert's account of his long trip, which included the crossing of Ellesmere Island. Herbert undertook this crossing as a training exercise, in preparation for his larger Arctic traverse to the Geographical Pole. He wrote:

"We were committing ourselves to a journey tougher than any we had previously experienced, a journey from which there could be no turning back, for the whole point was to test our metal, our technique, and our equipment over a course that

would either break us or prove we had the measure of ourselves
and our methods."

To my mind Herbert's assessment of this area was a real dampener.
Wally Herbert is undoubtedly Britain's foremost polar explorer, and
arguably the first man ever to reach the North Pole. If these were the
difficulties he had experienced with a dog team, what hope for a solo
trip? Otto Sverdrup, who in April 1899 had found the crossing equally
traumatic, wrote:

"The river fell in a deep waterfall into a canyon. We made an
attempt to get down here; and crossed a large drift of snow into
a fissure with perpendicular walls on both sides, the fissure
became deeper and deeper the farther we went and at last we
saw nothing . . ."

It occurred to me that this could be the ideal testing ground for a
comparison between dog travel and man-hauling. Dogs serve you well
whilst the terrain allows them to pull the sledges, but, should there be
problems, you have to man-haul everything. A man, on the other hand,
can easily pull a small paulk through restrictions at double the speed.
However, the time scale would be all important. It was a question of
having to rely on the dreaded support, or assessing the possibility of
going the whole way unsupported. Weight was going to be a critical
factor.

Looking at crossing Ellesmere from Eureka by the Sverdrup Pass,
as Wally Herbert, Cook and Sverdrup had, drew me to the conclusion
that it was, quite frankly, a horrendous prospect. Taking the Northerly

34

route through Canyon Fjord and across several glaciers looked in some respects the easier option: a shorter distance, no narrow passes, but on the other hand more ice caps to ski over.

A telephone consultation with Wally Herbert produced some sound advice. He thought it could be done by the Sverdrup Pass, but he didn't have the latest information on the glaciers and ice caps.

I also talked to Colonel Croft and Lord Shackleton who had travelled in the vicinity of the Kane Basin, seeking their advice. They both warned me of the ice bridge that lay to the South, and the fact that the Kane Basin is never the same two years running. One year, the pack ice can be solid rubble; another produces good consolidated flat pans of ice. Records also show that occasionally it had failed to freeze, preventing the ice bridge forming and consequently leaving open water, which would be disastrous.

I was advised that the one person I should contact was Dr Geoffrey Hattersley-Smith. This man has spent vast amounts of time mapping and travelling Ellesmere Island. He knew the area like the back of his hand.

We met at the Royal Geographical Society. Dr Hattersley-Smith is an impressive man, tall and proud, with hair like an eccentric professor. He came across as a person of great warmth and kindness. He listened intently as I outlined what I hoped to achieve.

We poured over the maps like teacher and pupil. "Look at this. Look at that. Did you know . . .?" and "By the way . . ." He had an unbelievable knowledge of the area and was willing to share it with me.

Finally I asked him straight, what were my chances of doing it solo, and which would be the best route to take?

In measured tones he said, "Well, looking at the route again, the glaciers on the Northern route could be very deeply creviced, and solo would be dangerous. Also, you would have to cross more land. Should this have no ice cover, and no river ice to follow, it would smash the base of your paulk to pieces." Further proof that it pays to talk to those who have experience – this was an insight that had not occurred to me.

He went on to say, "Of course, if you take Sverdrup Pass, it could be cut off by the glacier snout, but you could climb to the icefield and cross that way. If the Sverdrup Canyon is blocked, you could again climb out over the ice field.

"On balance, I would advise not to do it solo and secondly, if you do, to take the longer Southerly route through Sverdrup Pass."

I was to meet Dr Hattersley-Smith several times at the Foreign and Commonwealth Office where he works. A marvellous man to bounce ideas off, he was full of enthusiasm and knowledge. He had unknowingly become the father of the expedition.

It was at this stage that the project hit an unforeseen snag. My father suffered a heart attack. There were management problems in the company he was running and, for political reasons, I was asked to give up full-time expeditioning and join the board of directors. This new role very quickly became a full time occupation. In one sense, a new and demanding challenge, every bit as demanding as an Arctic Expedition.

Months slipped by, the expedition began to lose its priority, and gradually got put on to the back-burner. How could I possibly afford the time?

In due course, two other significant events in my life occurred: my marriage to Claire and, some time later in 1989, the birth of our first child. I still took the odd week to go climbing in order to keep fit and to maintain my commitment to the expedition, but my time was at a premium. As the years counted away my expedition files gradually got shifted from my desk to the top drawer of the filing cabinet, until they finally made their way to the bottom drawer, there to gather dust.

It was during a production meeting, that our receptionist put a call through from a Jock Wishart. After a few minutes' conversation, we agreed to meet up the next time I was in London.

At the appointed time I entered a London pub and spotted this individual parked in the corner. To me he looked a typical Scot. Gingerish hair, short and stocky, and built like a brick outhouse.

After an hour of social niceties concerning the weather, who he was, what I had done etc., he asked me if I wanted to join an expedition. Having sworn me to secrecy, he then went through the whole brief. His last words were, "I can't tell you exactly why I need this, but can you get four hundred gallons of fuel to the Geographical North Pole?"

I was intrigued. I said, "My God! Have you captured a Russian submarine or something?"

Having assured me that it was nothing quite that dramatic, he then asked if I would consider going to the Isle of Man to look at a project which was part of the expedition he was involved in. By this time, I was extremely interested. It transpired he wanted to get a new flying machine to the Pole. Shortly after the meeting with Jock I went to Neasden Airport to meet up with four other expedition members and advisors.

We were to fly over to the Isle of Man in a light airplane. As it turned out, the weather was disgusting: low visibility, heavy rain and thunderstorms, with high winds. I wasn't so sure I liked this excursion any more. I had had my moments with light airplanes before in the Arctic and on Mount McKinley, and it has led me to prefer 'planes with drinks on tap and long legs in the gangway.

We took off. I immediately pulled my seat belt so tight it was rupturing me. The sweat started to trickle down from my forehead, and I was developing cramps in my hands from holding on so tight. As we hit another air pocket and dropped another fifty feet, I was becoming a little worried. I thought, "Please don't let me be sick."

The Pilot looked back with a smile. "Everyone OK? Unfortunately, we'll have this all the way to Blackpool."

My esteemed companions didn't appear to notice my uneasiness. Sandy Woodward slept in the back, oblivious to any turbulence. Richard Burns just happened to be an ex-test pilot for the Harrier jump jet. The others were whooping it up with delight.

We landed in Blackpool for customs clearance before the second stage of the flight. My legs were wobbly and I was wet with sweat. I really wasn't sure if I wanted to go any further, especially when the forecast was for even worse weather. I quietly asked if there were any commercial flights over to the Isle of Man.

They all looked at me as if they were viewing a zombie. "You don't like this bad weather? Do you realise we have to go for years before we get bad weather this good?"

Obviously, there was going to be absolutely no chance of back-pedalling. Savouring the thought that, if I survived to see Jock again, I would throttle his thick Scottish neck until I squeezed an equal amount of sweat out of him, I fortified myself for the rest of the journey.

We landed safely, and there followed discussion after discussion concerning the project. I had forgotten so much. It had been a long time since I had been to the Arctic, and several years since I had slept on pack ice. I now had a comfortable job, with all the trappings of domestic life. Getting involved in this project gradually got me revved up again for dealing with the Arctic.

Up until now it was only Bob Swan's 1986 Antarctic expedition "In the Footsteps of Scott" that had revived any memories of that god-forsaken cold. He had just reached the South Pole to find that he had lost his ship. At the time I spent several days defending his expedition, which was truly an inspiration to thousands. My heart bled for him. It was a cruel blow to have success and bad luck in the same day, and it seemed to me the media gave him an unnecessarily hard time over the rescue of the ship's crew.

I suddenly thought, "Do I really want to do this expedition with Jock? Do I really need the hassle?" I mentioned this to Jock, who in his inimitable way, summed it up.

"Harry Truman once said, 'If you can't stand the heat, get out of the kitchen'."

Not entirely convinced, I kept with it. My task was to give the pilots ambient temperatures, emergency routes, pack ice information, emergency clothing lists. Other questions had to be addressed. How cold is the water? What thickness is the ice? How much open water in July? How many calories per day does a person need? What is the minimum emergency gear? What is the minimum weight? The challenge had started to fire me up once again. Slowly, but surely, I was becoming engrossed in the Arctic once again. I was beginning to miss it.

I had met Ray Shaw several times before on business. Half-Italian, half-English, he was forty-three, five feet eight inches tall, stocky, and going thin on top. He was probably, the most intelligent man I know, with a Ph.D. in Chemistry and an MBA from the London Business School. We also met socially, and on one occasion were enjoying an hour of relaxation when, after my second pint, he asked a question he had put to me a number of times before. "Why don't we do a Polar expedition together?" He was full of enthusiasm.

"We don't do it because it's horrible. Horrible weather, horrible food, horribly expensive, and horribly time-consuming."

Not a person to be easily put off, he went on and on and on. He was like a little school boy. The conversation continued along the following lines:

"Why not?"

"No!"

"Why not?"

"Because you haven't got any experience and I don't want a repeat of the 1983 Geographical Pole expedition. I made that mistake once – only a fool does it twice."

"How about another training trip before the big one, or an expedition which is equally testing but cheaper?"

"Well, there's always the Geomagnetic Pole."

This half-Italian suddenly sat up and started to get very excited. I slowly talked about the route and the problems.

"Brilliant! Brilliant! – how about it?"

"No."

"Why not?"

"Because we need a good scientific base, and I can't afford the time to do it."

"I'll do it."

"We'd need someone to go up early to sort out the base."

"I'll do it."

"We need money."

"I'll get it. So how about it?"

"No."

"Why not?"

"Because we'd need a good team."

"Well, you climb with Mitch and Steve, why don't you ask them?"

My determined objection to the idea began to waver. I could feel myself gradually being drawn into his excitement. It had never occurred to me to take a team to the Geomagnetic Pole as a training exercise for the Geographical Pole attempt. Looking at it objectively, the Geomagnetic Pole would be equally difficult, with the same problems, as pointed out by Wally Herbert, as going to the Geographical Pole. In fact, Wally Herbert's crossing of the Arctic Ocean sounded positively tame in comparison with his traverse of Ellesmere Island.

It was by now three in the morning. "Look, Ray," I said, "go home, think about it, and let's both sleep on it. Ask your wife, and call me tomorrow at twelve noon and I'll give you an answer."

A telephone call came at nine o'clock the next morning. It was Ray. He made it short and to the point. "How about it?"

"OK! On the condition that you get together a research programme, you go up early, and you put a lot of time into this." An Italian maniac was yelling on the other end of the telephone.

It was January 1990. I knew from experience we would soon get bogged down with the planning of the expedition. When you organise an expedition full time, you have the luxury of becoming totally absorbed in the business at hand, and are able to meet any person at the drop of a hat. The reverse happens when you have a full time job. You have to arrange meetings around the schedule of the working day. Expedition planning starts after 5.00 p.m. and goes on until late.

Ray contacted a number of universities around the country, undertaking the research. One of our objectives was to do the Royal Geographical Charter – "The Advancement of Geographical Science" – in an attempt to get RGS approval.

I listed out a budget of expenses in terms of equipment and finance. Within a short space of time, we had an excellent response. Due to past contacts in the equipment and business worlds, we reached our budget within one month. Eric Rose, the senior commercial business manager at National Westminster Bank, was a Dutch Uncle. We put some money on the money market, some on high interest related accounts and deposited some into currency fluctuation contracts for the purchase of anything we should need in Canadian dollars.

We contacted the Canadians and managed to get charts of the whole route with contours every five hundred feet. We even had satellite photographs of some of the route. The most amazing photos were the thermographs supplied by the Ice Climatology Division. These showed the pack ice and open water, even the thickness of pack ice, and a percentage breakdown of the pack's consolidation was discernible.

If Peary could see these photographs – they showed a lovely definition of the ice bridge crossing Smith Sound, with firm pack ice behind. We scheduled an update and brief every two months.

Choosing the team was in some ways the easiest, and in others, the hardest task. Having lots of would-be explorers contacting me to get involved in expeditions, I tend to take the easy option of trying to persuade friends who I think would be suitable.

My initial approach was to Steve Vincent. He's always first on the list, even though I am certain his answer will be no. Ever hopeful that he might one day say yes, I don't want him to think that he's forgotten. Like so many men, having got married, he settled down, and became positively respectable – only getting drunk when he sees me! In my opinion, this country lost one of the best explorers/adventurers to come out of the British Isles. His qualities far surpass any I might possess. He taught me my limited patience, and to see that there is nearly always another side to any story. It was he who showed me how to enjoy adventure, and enabled me to experience different cultures. Despite my Van Gogh's ear, he even managed to pass on some of his musical knowledge. I 'phoned him at work, the Dresdner Bank. "How about a holiday?" He knew me too well. Before I could even get into full flow the questions started coming.

"Where, how long, and when?"

"April 1991, one month, Geomagnetic Pole."

"Sorry, Kathy's pregnant and it wouldn't be fair."

Captain Richard Mitchell was next. Mitch was based in Germany, an Army Officer, flying helicopters. In some respects, he had superseded Steve in my travels around the world. Tall at six foot three inches, and athletic, Mitch always introduced a competitive edge to everything we did – we fed off each other. As a high-flying officer cadet, he won the Sword of Honour for best officer on his Sandhurst training course, gained an excellent degree from Shivenham Royal Military College of Science, graduated best pilot from the Army Air Corps and was able to outrun and drink me into the ground. We had now known each other for six years. Together, climbing and running, we had travelled extensively, and become very close. A relationship which has resulted in us being God-parents to each other's children.

Time and experience has taught our wives to expect their respective mates to be in some sort of trouble when the opposite number "hoves to" over the horizon. We do tend to get each other in trouble, doing more demanding things that we might not normally attempt as individuals. Jackie is an amazing lady, able to look after three children, cook and clean for the family, undertake the many duties of an Army officer's wife, and still find time to run her own thriving business.

I telephoned Mitch. "How about a holiday?" I went through the details.

"Game on," he said.

"But tell Jackie we'll only be away for three weeks."

The other member of the team, Steve Morris, had been to the Arctic twice with me, both times as a back-room boy. He was now in his late forties, tall, fit, and balding, and had just hitched up with a foxy young lady. He has a wonderful sense of humour.

I met him in a pub, and went through the pros and cons. He said he would like to go, but not to film, as he felt the conditions would be too harsh for video.

The walking team had been chosen: myself, Ray, Mitch, and Steve. I asked Jack Napper, who had been my main sponsor on the Magnetic Pole trip, to come up again and help man the radio. I enjoyed his company immensely and admired his skill at getting things done.

David Schofield was the last of the party, a young man whom I had come across in my business dealings at Ciba-Geigy. I was most impressed with his eagerness and his thoroughness in everything he did. He would be ideal to help Jack with the radios at base. The team was now complete.

Ray and I met every week to give an up-date on the planning, and we all met once a month at the Cricketers Arms at Littlewick Green.

By now Ray was well engrossed in our scientific work. He had spent a whole year putting together research projects to do on the trip and had arranged for eminent professors abroad, doctors from Universities and Institutions to be our supervisors.

We had a geology reconnaissance study supervised by Professor Dineley from Bristol University, a magnetometer study by Dr Barraclough of the British Geological Survey, a polymer study by Dr Mike Robbins from Ciba-Geigy, and a medical sleep study by Professor Keating and Dr James.

Ray put the expedition into the RGS for approval. He said, "No sweat." I tried to calm his excitement down. Wally Herbert, Vivien Fuchs, Ran Fiennes and Bob Swan all had problems getting approval. You don't get it because you are a nice guy. My success so far at the RGS had been abysmal. The first time I had been turned down because I didn't have enough experience. The next time had been because it was a solo expedition, and a subsequent expedition because I did not have a structured research project.

Ray 'phoned me up, swearing, cursing, half in Italian, half in English. We didn't get approval because we had too much research to do in the limited time available.

In retrospect, each time I have come back from the Arctic, I have always found these wise old men at the RGS to be quite correct in their evaluation. With hindsight, it was to become apparent that their assessment of our over-optimism was justified.

In company with Ray and Dave Schofield, I met Nigel de Windsor at the RGS. He was tremendously encouraging and put Ray in a better frame of mind.

We were now coming into Autumn 1990. Gradually, things started to fall apart in front of my eyes. Saddam Hussein was being naughty. The ice thermographs were still coming in with no sign of an ice bridge. It was late, and by now the ice should have been consolidated. I had a message from Schofield to meet him. He wanted to pull out of the expedition because he had just been promoted, and he felt Ray would come back in a body bag. He promised to pay for his own pre-paid air fare and expenses and shook hands with everyone. He was off the team. Our sponsor, Jack Napper, was going through headaches with his company. He had decided to sell, with the completion of the sale to coincide with his retirement, a date smack in the middle of the proposed expedition. If he didn't structure it carefully, he could lose a vast sum of money.

Kuwait was invaded and Mitch's unit became part of the UN force and was posted to the Gulf. Steve Morris was sent to the Gulf to do the filming.

I met Ray in London. Should we call it off? No! He was still full of enthusiasm. We met Lord Shackleton, who gave a shot of adrenaline to our expedition. "People may come and go, but keep to your objectives."

I was having my navigation updated by Derek Walters again. He had taught me everything about navigation for all of my trips, and had the patience of Job. Since the early days of sextant and starshots, GPS – Global Positioning System – had been introduced, with the ability to plot a position within three metres; it made things considerably easier. However, I needed to do the back-up on sextant in case the GPS should fail.

By chance, I then met Hugh Ward, an Army officer in the Engineers, whose wife worked for me in the Robnor laboratory. He had become increasingly involved with the expedition. I showed him the thermograph of the open water. "No problem," he said. "A small dinghy will do."

The thought of being in a little rubber dinghy, holed and sinking in the middle of sixty miles of open water, travelling at ten miles per hour with ambient temperatures of -40°C, and a life expectancy in the water of a couple of seconds, was something I did not want to contemplate. Hugh, on the other hand, was supremely confident. I instantly liked his can-do attitude. Unfortunately, he too might have to go to the Gulf, where the situation was daily becoming more serious.

Pete Praine was another back-room boy who had gradually become immersed in the excitement of the expedition. When Schofield backed out, he said immediately he would like to operate the radios. As a yachting enthusiast, he had a vast knowledge of radios and navigation, so I had no hesitation in welcoming him with open arms.

On January 15, 1991, everything seemed to pale into insignificance. As I had friends in the Gulf, I followed the progress of the war avidly. I read with trepidation the predictions of nerve gasses, biological warfare, the possibilities of limited nuclear war, and the shipment of thousands of empty body bags in readiness.

Last minute advice to Ray as he set off for Resolute from Gatwick, "Don't forget to cover your nose. Don't touch any metal with bare hands. Don't test the stoves in the tent." Don't, don't, don't. I was like a mother hen. "And don't get picked up by strange women!"

Ray 'phoned as soon as he reached Resolute. "It's a little cold, to say the least." He had been to the weather station and obtained an updated ice thermograph. The idea was that if the ice was OK, I would fly out with Pete, and if the ice had become any worse, the only money wasted would be Ray's air fare.

Ray told us that, although the ice conditions were not perfect, he didn't think we would have a problem, so, in April, I kissed Claire and Alicia good-bye and set off. It was the first time I had left my "family", and it was difficult. I can understand men giving up adventure for their loved ones.

It seemed strange to be going to Canada without Mitch. We had talked and planned for so long. We made the flight to Toronto, on to Edmonton and stayed the night. On to Yellowknife the next day in the usual Boeing 727, a small jet split half and half, cargo up front and passengers in the rear.

I was walking around the airport lounge at Yellowknife stretching my legs, when amazingly enough, I spotted Jim Merritt walking across the departure lounge. Pete Praine thought we were mad, standing there slapping each other on the back. It had been a long time since we last met up. Jim was now flying jets, instead of Twin Otters. He asked what I was doing. I explained about the polar trip to the Kane Basin.

"Shit! I did a lot of flying in that area for research for a Swiss scientist. He was trying to work out why so much open water appears in the Smith Sound before anywhere else at the same latitude."

In Jim's opinion, we should take the next plane home. This was a real blow. Out of all the people I know, Jim is the most optimistic. He said we had a much better chance of getting to the Geographical Pole than the Geomagnetic, because of the problems of open water.

I flew the second leg in a slight stupor. This advice was not from a man behind a desk looking at pictures from thousands of miles away, but from a man who lived and breathed the Arctic.

The 'plane circled Resolute. It was lovely to be back. Everything looked exactly the same. I stood at the top of the aircraft steps and, as always, the cold hit me like a brick wall.

Inside the departure lounge, it seemed that the whole village had come out to visit the newcomers. Bezal Jesudason was the first man I recognised from old.

Bezal is the personification of Norman Tebbitt's philosophy, "Get on your bike and get a job." Born in Bombay, he came to Canada to work and finally ended up in Resolute Bay, where he started "High Arctic Services", an organisation which is akin to a trekking company in the Himalayas. He will offer full board, equipment, tours to the North Pole by 'plane, and tours to see the wildlife of the Arctic. In addition he has a vast knowledge of the pack ice and the equipment you need. Suffice it to say, if you are serious in reaching any Pole, don't attempt to go without first consulting Bezal.

Ray had already hired the radio, rifle and Argos from him for our trip. In reply to my questions on how things were, Bezal said he had just flown back from Greenland, and the Kane Basin didn't look brilliant.

Resolute "Airport" is something of a misnomer. In reality, it consists of a wooden shed placed by the side of a runway. Looking out of the door you are faced with a road that passes between other wooden shacks owned by various departments that help keep a presence in the Arctic. If it wasn't for the stark cold air and total covering of snow and ice, you could well imagine this place being in the middle of the Wild West, where you tie your horse to a front rail. It is, indeed, a frontier town, for one of the last great wildernesses for mankind.

Pulling my coat hood over my head I walked down to the weather station. Although I was very weary, I could not rest until I knew what the update was. Ray introduced me to Glen Bond, the officer in charge of forecasting, with whom he had already built up a good rapport. Glen had at least twenty satellite photographs and thermographs in front of him, showing the Kane Basin. They revealed quite a distinct fracture zone.

I told him our plan was to get to the end of Bach Peninsula, head North along Cape Prescott, Dobbin Bay, and Cape Fraser, and then head South keeping on firm ice. He looked sceptical, but said he was awaiting two important updates on thermographs, and would give us a run-down in the morning. In the tent outside, Ray, Pete and I discussed the situation at length into the small hours of the night. We decided to try and get acclimatised quickly.

That night, none of us slept well. We were all troubled by indecision, worry, compromise, and just plain anger that of all the years, we chose the year that open water could occur! We got up at 6.00 a.m., decided to carry on as if we were still going, and booked the 'plane to take us up to Eureka in two days' time.

While Pete and Ray were packing all the equipment, I went over to meet the Director of the Polar Continental Shelf Project. These were the experts of the Arctic. I first talked to Leif Lundgard, a Polar

Shelf worker with donkeys' years of experience, whom I had known from past visits. I showed him the thermagraphics. He shook his head.

"You'll be swimming."

"We have a small boat with an outboard."

"But the current is twenty-four miles a day. You'd need an Ocean Liner," he said.

I talked to Jerry, the Director who also looked at the thermographs.

"You'll never do it. By the time you get to Bach, in fifteen days' time, nothing will be left of the ice."

I walked back to the hut to fetch Ray and Pete and take them to the weather station. I neglected to tell them what I had been told as I didn't want to pre-empt the meeting. It was a sullen group that went over to see Glen. Glen Bond worked in a building the entrance of which was similar to an air-lock. Consisting of an outer and inner door, this entrance served to keep out the cold air. Once through the second door you are immediately hit by the heat. Oppressive. Everybody walks around in T-shirts. Dressed in multiple layers for the outdoors, you soon start to roast. The next ten minutes are spent stripping down, taking care to stuff your gloves into your pockets. It's so easy to lose a vital part of your clothing.

We all sat around the table and listened to Glen.

"Well, boys, it looks worse. More ice has broken off, and is heading South. The bottom line is this. Suppose you start today. First of all, if you get to the Bach Peninsula and use a small boat to cross the water, will the Pole still be iced over? It's an important consideration, as the pick-up has to be carried out by an Otter fitted with skis, not floats. Secondly, in fifteen to twenty days' time when

51

you get to the edge of the present water, what do you think the ice conditions will be?" We all nodded like donkeys.

"Well, boys," he continued, rummaging through bits of paper, "this was the area fifteen days ago, ten days ago, five days ago, and today's situation. The whole area is very unstable, and moving fast. My belief is that the Pole will be under water by the time you get to Bach, and also the Neares Strait will clear of ice, so you'll have to use the boat again to get to the Pole and back to firm ice."

Ray was, as ever, optimistic, "Well, how about that? Sounds OK to me."

"Our sledges already weigh one hundred and sixty pounds each," I said. "A boat and outboard equipment would double the weight. No way could we manhandle it the whole way."

"How about getting to the end of Bach and using it as a training trip?"

I went off to the toilet to think. It's the best place to think privately (sometimes I think my brains are in my backside).

Considering the use of a boat had recalled a previous expedition involving a canoe trip round Cape Horn. The objective had been to complete a circular route along the lines of Jim Hargreaves' Cape Horn expedition, and to be the first to travel solo without support. However, on reaching the jump-off point, Porto Williams, I had been told it had already been soloed once by an American and once by a German. In any case, I would not be able to do it solo because of tensions between Chile and Argentina concerning the Beagle Channel. If I wanted to go South, I would have to do so with a naval minesweeper as escort. To top it all, the circular route was out of bounds because of new naval installations. Consequently, none of the objectives of the solo Cape

Horn Expedition were achievable. That trip hadn't been a success because none of the objectives were accomplished, nor was it a failure because we didn't actually attempt to achieve the objectives. However, I was lambasted in the Press, who represented me as a tourist who went to the end of Cape Horn, launched a canoe into the swell, and set off accompanied by a naval minesweeper escort on one side, and a rubber dinghy on the other. Everyone seemed to have an opinion as to whether I had succeeded or failed. In the event, I did neither.

I came back from the toilet and told the others, "No! The trip is postponed until next year." Geoff Birtles and Ian Walker, my biggest critics, had subconsciously taught me a very important lesson.

CHAPTER THREE

THE INNOCENCE OF THE LAMBS

After a week at home I was ready to go again. The Arctic bug had well and truly got to me. Feeling restless, I went into work and made a list of things to do for the following year. Luckily, most of the organisation had been completed, but we still had to gear up as if it was a new expedition to the Geomagnetic Pole.

I talked to Ray on the 'phone. He was pretty disillusioned, fed up with work and fed up with England. He decided he had had enough and was going to live in Italy.

"What about next year's trip?"

"I'm not sure."

Our roles had been reversed. I was the one all fired up, and he was committed to his family. At least he had seen part of the world most people don't see. As he said, "Once you experience a -40°C crap, it changes your outlook on life."

Pete Praine made an attempt to come back into the squad, only to discover after a short period of time, that one of his companies was going through an upheaval. Consequently he was committed to dates which would spread into the time we would be away. So he backed out.

It was back to square one with a new team needed. This recurring problem was basically because everyone I chose was either a businessman, or in the Services. Each one had commitments that were vital to his career. It would only be by chance that all the team would be available at the right time.

Mitch, now safely back from the Gulf, 'phoned me as soon as I arrived back in the UK.

"How about next year?" I asked.

"Game on," he said.

I was happy that he was on board. With him as a team member, I knew that the expedition would be top notch. Now I had to find some other lads.

Hugh came in to the factory to see how things had gone on the expedition. I sat him down, told him I needed someone to sort out the kit, and asked him what he thought about going on the new trip. He was as keen as mustard. He had just come back from Norway having completed Arctic Training with the Marines. As Mitch was going to obtain the food – only because his life revolves around pints of Stella and food – I now had a strong team of three – Hugh, Mitch and myself.

I had known Neill Williams through business for some years, a tall mild-mannered man, with a weird sense of humour. We had been abroad together several times on joint business projects. On one particular occasion, the project we were working on was falling apart around our ears. Neill continued to be up-beat, did not complain, kept his cool, and remained incredibly polite to the point of annoyance. While I was kicking tables and letting loose on all and sundry, he was always the original Cool Joe. He was also supremely fit. I booked him into an annual "Tough Guy Race", which is twelve miles of running in mud and icy water. If anything tests you, this does. He enjoyed it so much he laughed most of the way around.

I went to see him on business. Over coffee he asked about the postponed trip, and said he wished he could do something like that. I immediately invited him to join the next venture. He had a character which would easily fit in with everyone else, and Hugh would be able to look after him. He was very hesitant at first, his main concern being his commitments as MD of Polycrown, but I was persuasive and he eventually agreed.

One thing that concerned me was the ice bridge. Would it be better to go in February, when it was dark and very cold, but which would guarantee ice in the Kane Basin? Or would it be easier to go from Thule, get to the Pole early before the ice broke up, then traverse to Eureka?

I contacted the Ice Climatology Unit again. They were excellent forecasters. They went back through twenty-five years of records to find the best time to go. The data revealed that it was very rare for the ice bridge not to form. When it does, it consolidates the ice in the Kane Basin, leaving no open water until early May when all of the ice drifts out of the basin. It was just plain bad luck that we happened to choose one of the very rare years. Approximately five out of the last twenty-five years had seen a failure of the bridge to form.

The Unit sent me an updated photograph and thermograph, and it was a complete contrast to the previous year. The bridge was rock-solid, with no ice movement. Once a month they sent me an update. Each month when the fax came through, I gulped, then had a look. Nothing changed. 10/10 consolidation, with no change expected until June. This meant we would not have to go at the coldest time. I chose the first week of April. Cold, but not unbearably cold. Hopefully, we wouldn't be sitting on a pan of ice that suddenly decided to take a tour of the North Atlantic.

I arranged a meeting at the Pheasant Pub in Chippenham with all of the lads, plus Jill, the daughter of one of our shareholders, who wanted to help with the organisation side. This would be our regular meeting place. Five pints of Stella and five sausage, egg and chips being our staple expedition planning diet. Mitch always sat in the same place, looking at the bar, with his neck veins sticking out.

We held one weekend meeting on the Marlborough Downs. Although I knew all the individuals, the other members of the team had yet to get to know each other. After walking fifteen miles at a gentle pace, we finished the exercise with an all-out two mile run. Jill took several months to get over it. Tony Rolls, who lives opposite me was given the task of getting me fit. He, Mitch and I entered for the eighty mile World Trail Championship, held along the South Downs. We all ran it in less than twenty hours which showed our training was working well.

Whilst I was bitterly disappointed at not going the year before, especially for Ray, I was becoming supremely confident in our chances this year. The team was first class, each complimented the other in skills. We were all fit and the conditions looked right.

Our equipment was now under-going fine tuning. We decided to use Fischer skis with a new fish scale finish on the base. These allow your skis to slide forward, then grip as soon as you transfer your weight to move the other ski. You would normally have to use heavy skins to stop from sliding on the spot. The new skis and bindings were probably a third of the weight of my own precious skis. As with my previous expeditions, bits and pieces came in from all over the world. Bindings from the USA, Mukluks from Canada, skis from Austria, sledges from Sweden.

One matter remained to be resolved. Did we want to conduct any research? Every time I had gone away, I had always come back convinced that the RGS were correct, for various reasons, in not giving approval. The last trip was no exception. Ray and Pete had taken all the equipment out on to the ice with us, but it soon became obvious that there was no way we would be able to undertake all the planned research. We would be pushed to do even half of it. Thankfully, the RGS screening panel consists of people who have actual practical experience, not people who claim to know the Arctic through theory. We thought it best to restrict our research to projects which would be relatively easy to achieve.

We chose the polymer study again. This needed no direct input by the team since the sledges were made from resin. All we had to do was to provide Dr Mike Robbins with a sample after we had murdered the sledge, kicked it and beaten it, in the course of dragging it around the Polar Ice.

A magnetometer study was chosen on the basis that we would be able to plot our position each day more accurately. All we had to do was switch this machine on and record the number and time. Simple enough even for Mitch to use, and he wouldn't be able to eat it if he got hungry.

The third and final research project was the photo-geological reconnaissance. This again would be relatively easy, on the basis we would be taking photographs en route anyway. We dropped all other research.

We were lucky in that by June most of the organisational details had been taken care of. I wanted to get a British Fire Arms Certificate. I could then hire a rifle in Resolute, thus avoiding the nightmare hassle

I had experienced each time I took a rifle on a 'plane from Gatwick. Each airline, each airport, each airplane, exactly the same pantomime . . . "Why? Where? When? What for?

"Shooting polar bears."

"Don't get fancy with me, sonny!"

"I'm not, it's for a North Pole trip."

"Any more sauce from you, and you'll be missing your flight."

Last year two police constables had come knocking at my door. They went through the application form line by line.

"What do you need the firearm for?"

I knew this was going to be difficult.

"Shooting polar bears."

They looked at each other, then one of them said, "This is a very serious matter. Application for a firearm is taken very seriously. The individual's character is taken into consideration."

Being flippant wouldn't help my case, so I went to great lengths to explain. They both saw the funny side and thought the Chief Constable might give a double take when signing.

Mitch 'phoned up one night in July. "If we're going away in April, how about taking the families on holiday to Germany?"

"Why not to Switzerland?"

"Why not Zermatt?"

We both knew the area well and there would be an opportunity to try and get fit on the Matterhorn. We booked up a large apartment and drove over.

It was strange being back in our old haunts with our wives and children, and even stranger doing the tourist bit instead of roughing it. Needless to say, Mitch and I eventually got itchy feet, and the girls let us have one day off the lead by ourselves. We decided on the Matterhorn – though the girls would only let us do the normal route.

That evening we rushed up to the Hornli Hut, kipped, and Mitch woke me up at 2.00 a.m.

"Mitch, go back to sleep, we can follow the other people's head-torches later on. If we start now, we're going to be trail finding. If we follow everyone else, we can sleep for another two hours."

"OK."

Ten minutes later, "Ready now?"

"No."

He started to pull me from my bunk. I was playing for time, he wanted to get going. "Mitch, I need the bog."

While sitting on the throne, Mitch came in. "Come on, come on."

Downstairs, I said, "I need something to eat."

He shoved three rolls into my pocket, "Come on, come on."

I felt sick from tiredness. We crunched outside, our head-torches flickering on the footprints in the snow. We followed them up to a huge black rock face.

"Go on then, Mitch."

"No way, you lead."

The climb was supposed to be a grade II but I was struggling after ten feet.

"Jesus, hurry up."

"Mitch, this is bloody hard. Are you sure this is the route?"

"Get going, you big pussy. You're slow because of the altitude."

I thought, "This isn't altitude problems."

I inched my way up. No protection whatsoever. I couldn't see Mitch. His head-torch was off.

"Mitch, this is no way a grade II. This is a bloody V, without protection."

I found a stance and told him to come up. Half an hour later, he said, "That's the hardest climbing I've ever done." Just then a stream of head-torches came to the bottom of the face and traversed left, completely away from our route. We had wasted two hours on the wrong route.

"You twit. I told you we should have waited."

We had nothing to abseil from back to the route. This was turning into a nightmare. I traversed around on to easier rock, and then got back down on to the route. More time lost! We had not even started and we were already running out of time. Mitch had promised Jackie we would be back by 6.00 p.m. Was it worth trying? We decided to give it a go.

Once we were on the proper route, we went storming up. Unfortunately, the Matterhorn is so popular you sometimes get upward of fifty pairs going up. We reached the tail-enders and started to overtake people. By the time we reached the Solvay Hut on the Mosley Slabs, a real bottleneck had developed. We hung around for an hour. No one would let us pass. We gradually got higher, until we were experiencing a double bottleneck: people waiting to go up were meeting people coming down. It was a nightmare. I had climbed this route in early Spring once before, and had no problem. This was

61

climbing at its worst. Notwithstanding the fact it was marvellous to see so many people on the mountain, the delays were causing tempers to fray and it detracted from the beauty of the scenery.

We eventually reached the shoulder. The queue stretched up in front of us. We looked at our watches. We both thought of Jackie. If we didn't get down on time, a little red rescue helicopter would soon be buzzing around. We raced down, missed the cable car, so ran down into Zermatt. It had been lovely to have a day out.

A regular routine of preparation concerning the expedition soon developed. Time sped by very quickly.

Each month we received a satellite thermograph of the ice and held a planning meeting to iron out the details we still had to attend to. Most of the equipment was now in, and we had promises for most of the sponsorship money.

On the basis it would cover any contingencies, I was anxious to obtain a major sponsor. The first person I contacted was Jim May of Advantek, Robnorganic's agents in America, who also have a thriving industry selling a product to the electronics market around the world. Jim had recently been in the UK visiting my father, who has been a friend and business colleague for many years. It was during this visit that Jim expressed interest in our trip. Later, we talked at length on the 'phone, and he agreed to become our major sponsor. At that time, I felt it would be nice to take someone from Advantek on the actual expedition. I knew Jim's son Jeff well. He was about my age, and in the same position as me working with his father. A very bright guy and a fine athlete who had a good sense of humour. I talked to him at length, but he felt his business commitments just wouldn't give him the time.

I wrote to Jim asking if he had, in the Advantek organisation, a deaf and dumb blonde nymphomaniac who was a good cook, who might like to join us. A day later I had a fax saying they had someone. I thought, "Boy, things are looking up." Her name was Tamara Sarrack.

I talked to the lads about the new recruit, but it went down like a lead balloon. There had been a lot of talk recently about the "buddy system", and the dangers of factions building amongst the team members. When you are in a hostile environment, you use the buddy system to look out for each other, in particular when it's cold to see frostbite on your extremities that you wouldn't normally see. However, this sometimes leads to two distinct teams, and occasionally, hassle between them. Taking someone from Advantek would have given an odd number which would help alleviate the problem, but a female on the team they thought would be disastrous, everyone falling over each other to help. I remember when we were in Eureka on the Geographical Pole trip, the ugliest woman I have ever seen came in as a weather tech. Within days, the pilots and weather men were fighting over her! What the hell would happen if she was good looking?

I wrote to Jim to explain that I thought it might be best if she worked the radios at base for one year and, if she was good, we would look at the situation again on the next trip. Jim came back in agreement and asked if his daughter Elaine could accompany her and help in Resolute. This presented no problem to us, so we agreed.

Later Tamara had to drop out, so Elaine wrote asking if Shirley Chenoweth could come up. Having met Shirley before a couple of times, I knew she would be just fine on the trip. We agreed to all meet up in Montreal on the way up to Resolute. We sent fax after fax detailing kit for the women to bring up from Minnesota, as they would be staying a long time in a cold, strange and hostile environment.

We were still worried about the pairing up problem. Now we had a major sponsor, I was keen to give full value for money. Jock Wishart was the ideal man. We needed someone of his calibre to be on the trip. Not only was he familiar with the way in which the media works, he would also be an asset to the team.

We often met for lunch, and this day we went to a Thai restaurant. I told him about the trip, the route, and the conditions. How easy it would be for him.

I said, "Jock, this will be a walk in the park for a man like you."

"Hmm, hmm, very interesting. I'll let you know. Hmm, very interesting."

He 'phoned up as usual at 8.00 a.m. "OK, I'm in. But I'm very limited on time, as I have to go to Singapore on business. I have a maximum of twenty-five days."

We all met up at Robnorganic one Saturday. The expedition was now getting too close for comfort. Again the ice looked good. It was January, and we now had precious little time. The whole day was spent sorting out food and equipment. We had the best equipment on the market. Mitch and Hugh thought it was Christmas with all the free kit, opening up new Aztec sleeping bags like excited little boys.

We also assigned each person to his duties. Because of his previous Arctic training, Hugh would be responsible for cooking and for looking after Jock and Neill, the rookies of the trip. Neill and Jock would be responsible for the camp administration, sorting out tents, and the camp in general. Mitch and I would do the research projects, set the radio and Argos up, and do all the navigation. Jock would naturally look after the PR, with the help of Jill Parry in England.

(top) Gatwick Airport Thursday lunch-time - we were on the
ice by Sunday lunch-time.
(above) Sorting out the equipment in Resolute.
(right) Jim May, our illustrious sponsor.

Unloading Twin Otter at Eureka

Walking down Eureka Sound - flat ice

A normal camp site.

Mitch taking magnetometer readings.

Jock and Neill eating from monster bags.

Inside a steamy tent.

That night we slept in a huge freezer owned by Farepak Hampers. The temperature dropped to -25°C. We all arrived with our mountains of kit. I made everyone walk into the deep freeze in their casual clothes. We then stripped down to our boxer shorts and quickly redressed in our cold weather gear. We put one tent up, and all crawled in. It was immediately evident that for the actual expedition we would need two tents. Neill and Jock, I thought, should go in with Hugh in the cooking tent as it would be warmer there and neither were experienced in cold weather. Mitch and I would have the cold unheated tent with the provision that if any pairing off started to occur we would re-jig the sleeping arrangements.

After half an hour Mitch was up and looking for food. "Do you think they would miss a frozen turkey?"

"We haven't got a stove, Mitch."

"Is there anything to eat?"

After twenty minutes, he went to the security office and asked for a cup of tea and sandwiches from the guards. It was a good lesson for Hugh as cook: Mitch has hollow legs, so Hugh would really have to keep the food coming thick and fast to satisfy him.

Jock wanted to start the ball rolling on press conferences, but unlike most sponsors, Jim wanted the minimum amount of fuss. This was a unique experience, quite unlike most expeditions. It was also a terrific advantage, as it didn't put any pressure on us.

We were now into the last week of March 1992 – and the last week of preparation time. Mitch had flown over from Germany and Hugh came up from Plymouth. As we would be pushed for time once we arrived at Eureka, we decided to sort out as much as possible in

England.

This last week was devoted to packing food, adjusting zips and buttons, and putting pockets on thermals. Mitch was not impressed by the food.

"We need more calories," he said. More chocolate was ordered. We were counting on eating 6000 calories a day.

Margaret, a Robnor secretary, was now full time secretary for the expedition. Engineers were making last-minute alterations. Drivers were dispatched to fetch last minute bits, and storemen were packing food. By now, nearly every one of the seventy Robnor staff had become involved in the expedition to some degree.

Over many years of going away I have learnt that good-byes should be quick – and at home. On April 2nd 1992, Mitch kissed Claire and Alicia and waited for me in the car. I kissed and hugged them both and left quickly. We met up with the rest of the team at Gatwick. I had told everyone to wear blazers and ties as we were going business class. We all lined up with masses of equipment: we looked like a bunch of clean-cut Mormons.

I had tried to tell the others to leave good-byes at home but only Mitch held the same opinion. I kept well away from Debbie, Jock's wife. She thought I was a fool for taking him, and that he was just plain stupid for going, especially as his daughter was so young. Hugh's wife was crying, and Neill's wife looked like a scared rabbit who had been caught in the headlights of a car. That look of total confusion and fright hurt me. She was with her parents and two children. I told her Neill wouldn't be going if we didn't think he was up to it. I promised to get him back safely.

For the first time in twenty years of travelling, I realised I was a leader responsible for men who had wives and children back home. I mustered enough courage to talk to Debbie. "I know he'll be OK. Don't worry."

Mitch and I left the others to it and found the departure lounge. They followed slowly, with stunned looks. No turning back now!

Not for the first time that day, Jock was soon on the 'phone making business calls. When the aeroplane door was closed Jock still wasn't on board. I asked the purser to give one more call. I would kill him if he missed the flight. A few minutes later, they re-opened the door and Jock sheepishly walked in. Neill asked him if the stock market had just crashed.

The team headed for Toronto in the lap of luxury, five men and thirty-two bags of luggage, including a satellite telephone, generator, two satellite tracking systems and a mass of other kit.

We arrived at the Sheraton Hotel in Montreal with all our kit intact and nothing lost. I had booked two rooms. Neill felt the hotel and flight were over the top for a bunch of bums. I told him he was now in the first division, but in fact we had been up-graded because of business contacts

Everything was going perfectly to plan. Even our mukluks were waiting for us. We stripped into jeans and our expedition sweaters and went upstairs to meet the two girls, who had arrived on an earlier flight.

The team politely introduced themselves and sat down for some American-style hospitality. Unaware that we only drank beer, Shirley was dishing out the whisky in double measures. Mitch and I tried to down them without touching our throats, so we wouldn't taste it. She

67

then gave us triples! The only solution was to retire to Montreal's Old Munich Beer Hall.

It was a great way to get to know them. Elaine, who was our age, was a highly intelligent lady waiting to go to medical school. Shirley was a housewife in her seventies from Minneapolis.

The two women would be looking after our welfare while we were on the ice. We inevitably got onto the subject of radio schedules, Argos readings, what procedure to follow if they didn't hear from us. Neill, Mitch, Jock and Hugh all listened intently. We were now discussing life and death decisions. It was gradually coming home to everyone that this was it! Expeditions are nine tenths planning and one tenth doing.

Boarding the aircraft, we all squeezed into our seats bound for Resolute. Over the intercom: "It is now −35°C in Resolute."

I looked at Mitch. "It should be −20°C!" I had come through Resolute many times, but it had never been that cold.

By the time the flight made a short stop at Frobisher Bay, everyone had gone very quiet. "We're committed now," I said to Neill. As the flight continued, the scenery gradually gave way to true Arctic tundra: pack ice between the islands, and beautiful mountain ranges. We circled Resolute, landed and taxied to a halt outside the Resolute Airport lounge.

I stood at the door. There was an overwhelming feeling of success in my bones. The team was the best, the equipment was the best, and, very importantly, the conditions were perfect.

The first blast of −35°C in your lungs changes all that. You ask yourself, "What the bloody hell am I doing here?"

Thursday 2nd April – Montreal
Elaine May's Journal

Tonight we met the team: four tall and fit young Brits and one short Scotsman. All uniformed in their expedition navy blue sweaters and blue jeans.

We did not see much of Jock tonight, he succumbed to jet lag and excused himself, but the rest of the team, accompanied by Shirley and me, moved to the Old Munich Beer Hall, where we got to know each other a little better. It was in this pleasant environment that Shirley and I began to learn exactly what our role and duties would be for the next four weeks.

Hugh and Mitch are both in the British Army. Mitch has flown reconnaissance in the war that Americans call the Desert Storm, but Brits (as we found out tonight) refer to as Operation Granby. Both have experienced cold weather conditions, Mitch having accompanied Kim on some mountaineering trips, and Hugh having completed the Army Arctic training. Neill is a very nice, soft spoken man who, although obviously fit, looks a little thin and pale compared to the others. He has not been on a similar trip before.

Because of the seating arrangements, I didn't get to speak to Kim, but he seems to be very congenial, making sure his team has enough beer and sausage, smiling at us with his friendly grin.

This is the last night of civilisation for all of us. For the team, the time is fast approaching when they will be on their own, out on the ice. Everyone is excited, but it is quite obvious they are a little scared underneath it all.

PART TWO

THE EXPEDITION - APRIL 1992

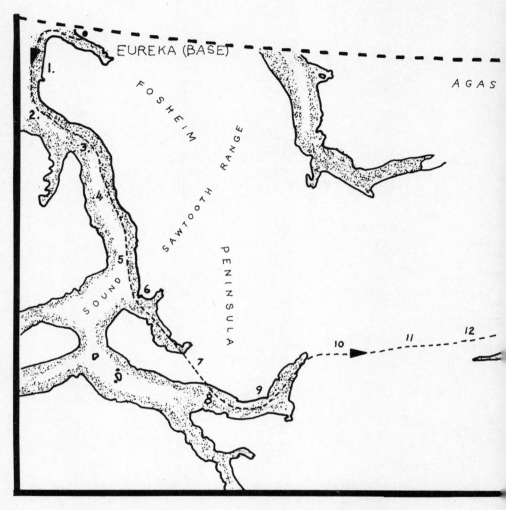

Map labels: EUREKA (BASE), FOSHEIM, SAWTOOTH RANGE, PENINSULA, SOUND, AGAS

ROUTE TAKEN FROM EUREKA TO THE GEOMAGNETIC POLE

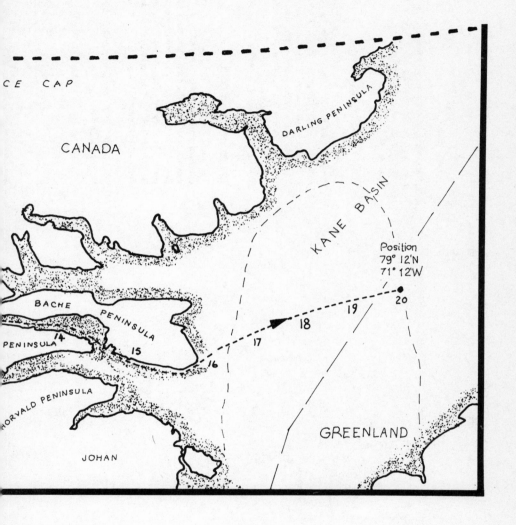

DIAGRAM TO SHOW THE RELATIVE POSITIONS OF
THE NORTH POLE, THE NORTH GEOMAGNETIC POLE AND THE MAGNETIC NORTH POLE

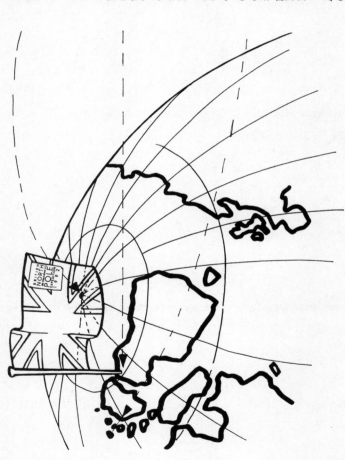

North Pole

The Earth spins once every 24 hours about its axis of rotation. The Geographical North Pole is the place where this axis meets the Earth's surface. Position 90° North.

North Geomagnetic Pole

A good approximation to the Earth's magnetic field is the field that would be produced by an extremely strong bar magnet placed at the Earth's centre and tilted at an angle of about 11° to the axis of rotation. The place, in the northern hemisphere, where the axis of this bar magnet, produced, meets the Earth's surface is the North Geomagnetic Pole.
Position 79°12' North 71°12' West.

Magnetic North Pole

The Earth's magnetic field has both strength and direction, the latter being measured by the angles of declination and dip. The point where the field direction is vertically downwards is the North Magnetic Dip-pole or, in everyday terms, the North Magnetic Pole. Here the dip is 90° and the declination is undefined.
Position 78° North 103° West.

Description and positions given by British Geological Survey

CHAPTER FOUR

HOME FROM HOME

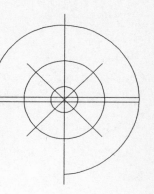

Friday 3rd April – Resolute

I walked down the steps and across the hundred yards to the airport building. Walking in, you came across a melee of people. For most of the village, the arrival of a 'plane is the highlight of the week. The sniff of an expedition is extra excitement. People look you up and down, and either say, "No way," or "Maybe."

They have seen a multitude of "nut cases" come through these parts, from the Japanese motorcyclist who put his rations in the handle bars, rode to the end of the runway and froze the engine, to the lady whose sole job on her expedition was to keep the butter from freezing by putting it in her bra. With what success has never been revealed.

I recognised people instantly, friends from before, such as Bezal and Terry, and people such as Joe, the Royal Canadian Mounted Policeman from the previous year. I looked around to see where the team was. Admittedly we were all dressed in jeans and shirts and had ordinary shoes on, but -60°C wind chill had certainly sobered us up, removing all trace of the effect of the welcoming drinks of the previous evening. The looks on the faces of both Neill and Jock were worth a million words. They were stunned and bewildered.

We quickly reclaimed our luggage and, for the first time ever, everything had turned up. It was a good omen. Everything was slipping into place. Elaine and Shirley boarded the Borek pick-up truck and went off to the pilot quarters that was to be their home for the duration of the trip.

Finally, everyone drifted out of the airport, and we were left in the middle of the lounge with all our kit. Five mad Brits out in the midday sun.

The words of Rudyard Kipling came to mind again, "If you can meet with triumph and disaster . . . " I wished I could print those words over the door of the airport lounge.

I stripped off and started to get changed. Gradually, without a word, everyone followed suit. We put all our kit in a pile and waited for the van. "OK, lads," I said, "it's 5.00 p.m. Resolute time, Friday night. On the assumption all kit is tried and packed, we'll fly out to Eureka Sunday lunch-time."

Tonight, we would get an update on ice and obtain the long range weather forecast. Sleeping in the hangar tonight at -8°C, would aid us to gradually acclimatise. We aimed to get some food at 9.00 p.m.

The van pulled up. We piled on to the truck, drove over to the hangar, rigged up some lights, moved aircraft wheels, tools etc., and made it "home from home". Hugh soon got the stove going, and brews came hot and fast.

I asked Hugh to give Neill and Jock another pep talk about frostbite and cold nip. In -60°C, you have little time to act, it must be instinctive. You can have permanent damage in seconds.

Jock said, "I thought it's supposed to be -20°C and lovely and warm. Warm my ass!" He was right. This was unexpected. I was really worried. If we lost someone through carelessness it would be a disaster.

"Look after each other. Don't get complacent," I warned them.

"Fine chance," quipped Jock.

Everybody was roaring around with lists of tasks. It was brilliant to see everyone working furiously, partly to keep warm, but partly to do the best for the team. Everyone was keen to carry out their duties.

I walked over to the weather station with Mitch and we introduced ourselves to the weather technicians. We were expected. Ice thermographs were already waiting for us. The Kane Basin was 10/10 consolidated. The bridge had crept slightly North, but was still forty miles away from our route. The long range weather forecast out of Eureka for Sunday was excellent. Cold but still.

I was feeling euphoric. Up to now everything was going to plan. The team were shaking down and gelling well together.

We walked over to see Elaine and Shirley at the pilot's quarters. As soon as I was through the door, I saw a huge nude photograph on the wall. Sheepishly I asked Elaine and Shirley if they would like to be moved to a more civilised place. "Hell no!" said Shirley, "My bedspread has frozen to the wall, and the toilets have blocked up, but this is fun!"

Bezal took us back to the hangar. He had brought the rifle, radio and Argos system. He was always amazingly helpful, slowly and carefully checking through the equipment for us. "If you are lucky, maybe this year," he said. I admired him immensely. Coming to the North with nothing, he had created a thriving business in an incredibly hostile environment. His success was entirely due to a great deal of hard work on his part. One wonders what he might achieve under normal conditions. Probably run Canada!

It was now growing late. Since we had landed three hours ago,

Mitch had complained every five minutes that he was hungry. I 'phoned up Narwhal, a small boarding house. How much would they charge for an evening meal? Thirty dollars a head. After haggling, I got it down to twenty dollars. It was probably the worst deal they had ever entered into. We all walked over, stripped all our outer clothes off, and settled in for action. Soup, followed by a mountain of food – potatoes, lamb chops, four veg – followed by a huge helping of pudding and a litre of milk. I couldn't move.

Mitch looked around, and then went through the whole three courses again. The chef looked on in disbelief as Mitch followed that off by eating half a loaf of toast. We waddled back.

Friday 3rd April – Montreal to Resolute
Hugh's Journal

This morning I awoke to Kim being impatient for the off. At 6.30 a.m. I got up and by 7.00 a.m. the group was on its way. All seemed to be going well until I was told to report to security with my clasp knife. Apparently I should have put it in my freight, and they have retained it until I return. Annoying!

We departed Montreal at 9.00 a.m. on a 737 bound for Frobisher Bay.

Weather beautiful, sun and blue skies with a temperature of -25°C and a ten mile per hour wind. Resolute is -35°C with a ten mile per hour wind. Very cold. Moved to workshops, temperature at -8°C is good for acclimatisation. The team are all keen to get working and help with the preparation. I check fuel calculations with Neill.

Saturday 4th April – Resolute

Saturday morning, Mitch woke us up again. He was hungry and had already made arrangements to eat at Narwhal. When we reached the door we started to undress. Mitch noticed Hugh had frostnip on his nose already. It was our first warning against complacency. We had only walked down the high street and this had happened.

After breakfast we still had lots to do. We all tried the rifle, Neill missed the target by a mile. (God help us if he had to shoot wildlife to keep us fed.) The radio, stove, Satcoms, were all now working perfectly. The only remaining problem was Jock's Satcoms Telephone. He had wanted to pull this device with its own generator so he could talk to the outside world. Although we all knew it was heavy, it had to be Jock who made the final decision. I don't think he relished the idea of the thing working for two days, then packing in. It would have been much too heavy to haul the whole way as dead weight. In the end, he kicked it and called it something in Scottish.

We went over the route again with Gregg, the Borek Station Manager. Shirley and Elaine went through the radio procedures, and the actual route we would be taking. They had to know what we were thinking if they couldn't contact us. Mitch went over the pick-up procedure one more time.

I decided it would be an idea to sleep out the last night. Jock wanted to check out his contact lenses, and it would help with acclimatisation.

We all slept badly due to apprehension. We were leaving in the morning. This was it. No turning back. I tossed and turned. Did we have everything? Would everyone be OK? Would the equipment be

OK? Would the ice hold? Would Sverdrup Pass be kind to us?

Mitch knew what I was thinking. "Get to sleep, you soft git. It won't get any better by worrying about it."

Saturday 4th April – Resolute

Neill's Journal

Today is Christian's birthday. Happy Birthday, little man X X X

A day of checking equipment and splitting up the load to be packed into the paulks.

The radio telephone Jock has hauled all this way will not operate in these temperatures.

Last night we slept in the back of the Borek workshop. Each of us using a single sleeping bag. It was -8°C, but the smell of aircraft fuel and lack of light were more of a problem than the cold. However, I slept more than I had expected as a non-camper.

We walked to Resolute Hamlet, a distance of about four and a half miles, in a temperature of -32°C which the wind-chill reduced to -45°C. This is very cold, you can feel it biting into you, conjuring up a mental picture of wolves' teeth.

Tonight we sleep in tents, and have been told to expect little or no sleep because it will be so cold. If we get through this OK, then we are off for the start tomorrow.

Fired the rifle today. I was the only one to hit the hill in the far distance. Everyone else missed and hit a stick that was in the line of fire.

I just want to get on with this. I would like a bit more to do and feel a need to be involved without appearing to be "pushy". I would hate any of the team to think they have to "carry" me.

Hope Christian had a good birthday party.

Saturday 4th April – Resolute

Jock's Journal

Day was spent checking equipment and splitting up the load into the various paulks. For a little bit of exercise, later on in the day we walked across to the Resolute Hamlet, which is about four and a half miles away. Temperatures were down to about -40°C – and that was very very cold. Hugh and Mitch started to stride out. Determined and competitive as always, I kept up the pace with them. I was not going to let these soldiers show that they were not the bees knees. For the first time we saw the skin of a polar bear: it really is quite awesome. The skin was stretched out over twelve feet. It gave me a little bit of concern, I would not like to meet one of these in a dark alley for sure. We walked back to the camp at a more gentle pace and got the rifle out – rather an old German make – which, as I found later, was going to have more use than just as a rifle. We all had a practice with a couple of bullets behind Resolute. The only one who managed to hit the post was Kim. So much for Army training.

CHAPTER FIVE

A WALK IN THE PARK

DAY 1 – Sunday 5th April

This morning we loaded all the kit on to the Twin Otter. Checklist after checklist was run through. Matches, lighter, spare sunglasses, spare bindings, wax, tool kit, radio spares, etc. etc. Three pages. Checked and double checked. It would be an expensive return trip if we forgot anything.

We started to load the 'plane. Elaine climbed up the ladder. Shirley couldn't quite get her leg on the first rung. Neill and Jock looked at her, said "Excuse us," grabbed a cheek each and pushed her in through the door.

The 'plane gathered speed, Mike pulled back on the joystick and we rose into the clear blue sky once more. The scenery was breathtaking. Fjords, lakes, mountains and cliffs, ice-fields and glaciers. Inside the aircraft, apart from the sound of the engine, all was quiet. Every one of us felt apprehensive. We had come a long way. Down below looked beautiful, but totally inhospitable. We all knew this wasn't going to be a holiday. I kept thinking of the wives, Lindsey, Jackie, Debbie, Yvonne and Claire. I had promised them all I would look after their husbands. I just hoped nature would be kind.

We landed at the cinder strip. Just outside was the hut we used as a base for my solo Geographical trip. Still standing was the wooden toilet shack where Mac – the radio operator – lost the skin off his backside after Steve and I removed the lining on the seat. Just across the way the mountain that looked like Table Mountain was visible. It seemed like yesterday since I was last here. Nothing had changed. We piled off the 'plane. The weather station had come up with a truck to take us the two miles to the station on the side of the fjord. The weather station was basically the same.

Elaine and Shirley

Being five reasonably fit, sun-tanned, raucous young men, we contrasted strangely with the group of very quiet, white, overweight weather techs. Wally Herbert wrote:

> " . . . the men of the station who came out to greet us were shaken and silent, for we were burned the colour of parchment, scabbed, and raw with frostbite sores."

I wondered what we would look like the other end when we got picked up.

It was now three in the afternoon. The filming completed, we hugged Elaine and Shirley and said our good-byes.

We were now alone.

I called the guys together and spoke to them. "If we can make it through the first five days, we can hack the trip. We have come here as a team. At times we will be tired, frightened and hungry. We will also get on each other's nerves, but we pass or fail as a team. One for all and all for one."

We shook each other's hands and started to walk. It was just three and a half days since we had left London.

In common with McMurdo base in the Antarctic, Eureka is a name that is synonymous with High Arctic adventure. Nearly all modern polar expeditions pass through this tiny dot on the map. Behind us, the collection of huts which made up the base, in front, our route.

It was -40°C with brilliant blue skies. We had to cross Slidre Fjord, hitting land the other side before traversing around until we came into Eureka Sound. It looked as if you could reach out and touch the other side, it was so crystal clear. Very similar to Alpine sunny days, but much colder.

We started off in single file. Within a very short space of time, we began to take clothing off. In theory, you should pace yourself carefully in order to prevent sweating. However, this was easier said than done: we were hauling sledges weighing one hundred and fifty pounds each and Mitch's was closer to two hundred pounds. It was heavy going and each team member strained into his harness. We had waxed the bases of the sledges until they slithered like a snake when empty. Loaded, it was like engaging in a tug-of-war with a bulldozer. Within the hour I was down to one thermal top and bottom and still sweating. It was quite a sight. The thermals were developed by Sub-Zero, designed to wick away the perspiration to the outer layer, leaving the wearer covered with a layer of frost. It worked perfectly. We looked like snowmen, trudging along with our worldly belongings.

It was a wonderful feeling to be finally on our way, a mixture of excitement and uneasiness. It wouldn't be easy, but if we were lucky we should be able to do it. Neill and Jock listened intently to any advice as we went along.

We stopped on the hour, checked each other out for white spots, brushed off all the frost, put a top coat on to keep the warmth in, then guzzled coffee from a flask. It was strange, that first stop. Everyone had a pee, each checking the colour of urine to see that it was healthy, not straw and yellow, indicating dehydration. Mitch and I knew each other well, but the others walked twenty yards away and turned their backs for solo performances. In the cold weather, you often need a cocktail stick to find your pecker, by which time you have done a war dance and peed down your trouser leg.

We seemed to be going at a tremendous pace, but the headland never came any closer. Distances are so deceptive in the Arctic. What looks like a molehill is sometimes higher than Snowdon. What looks like a short distance can be like walking across the Channel. For that very reason, I always walked by time, and not to a point or a given place.

Gradually, Eureka weather station was put behind us, and other mountains came into focus the other side of Eureka Sound. The bay was wonderfully flat. We had stowed our skis, as the ice was solid, and we didn't break through the top crust. The whole place seemed so sterile and clean, the light twinkled on the snow, and with each step came a crunch. Each man was silent, deep in his own thoughts. Only at the hourly stop did we break out of that mode. I kept thinking, "As long as we can get through the five day barrier." Psychologically, I find that imperative. By the time you have five days under your belt, you have got into a routine. Having survived that length of time, you start to build confidence in yourself. I looked back: a single file had been made with a sledge track, crisp and clean.

We hit land after four hours, and traversed around the coast. We were now out of sight of the weather station. I told the group, "Guys, one more hour, and we'll make camp at 6.00 p.m." I put Mitch in the lead, and he fired away, blazing the trail and giving us extra distance.

At the end of the day, I am usually knackered, and unless I concentrate during the last couple of hours, I make very little progress. With a strong team, I had plans to change the lead man at different times of the day, in order that we would continually have a fresh man at the front of the pack.

Mitch stopped. I had made Hugh camp administrator, so told him to get on organising the lads. We all had our individual tasks. Jock and Neill would put the tents up, get the food into the tent, and gather large black bags of snow to melt down for our drinks. I would roll out the radio dipoles. Mitch would do the magnetometer readings.

The first night, Hugh insisted on sleeping on land. No big deal really, but what happens when we are out of sight of land? I asked. It was very important not to make any big issue from this triviality, so we slept on the coast amongst the boulders.

We all snuggled into our sleeping bags. Mitch and I were in the cold tent, so Hugh passed our first large mug of tea through. What service! This was a new experience for me, used as I was to solo trips. With another shout of "Nosh," two huge plates of hot grub came under the tent door valence. We struggled out of the maggots and waffed the food down. I looked at Mitch and said, "I could eat that again."

"How about two pints of Stella and ham, egg and chips?"

I was just nodding off when the tent started to flap. The wind had started to blow. At least we could sleep through that, hopefully in the morning things would be honky dory.

Day 1 – Mitch's Journal

For the crew of the Twin Otter loading our equipment, this was just another day. Transporting Europeans, and vast amounts of equipment on one-way trips Northwards has become a commonplace activity. Whereas to all members of the expedition this was probably the most important day of the past year. All the preparation and work to get us this far would amount to nothing if we had made wrong decisions in the preparation and packing the equipment.

The last two days have been spent calculating fuel requirements, preparing the food and fine tuning the remainder of the stores. Whilst I was certain in my own mind we had the right type and quantity, a leak in the fuel, or a poor set of radio batteries could mean the difference between success and failure. As an unsupported expedition nobody would be able to help us even if we wanted them to.

The Chef at the local canteen knew we were off this morning and made the necessary adjustments. We ate for Britain – as the last mouthful of fried breakfast slipped down my throat I wondered how I was going to cope on the measly portions of food we had been packing earlier. On previous expeditions with Kim I've been able to supplement my diet by "trawling" the bread baskets on hotel and Refuge tables. This time there is to be no such luxury.

As Resolute Bay slipped below the wing of the Otter, my mind wandered and I relaxed in the knowledge that we had a peaceful three hour 'plane ride ahead of us. Two minutes later, I was disturbed in a manner that was to become the norm for the next three weeks – get yourself settled with the tour kit nicely stowed and THEN Kim wants a photograph taken! I spent the flight filming video and taking stills.

Stepping down from the aircraft at Eureka I deliberately pushed aside all thoughts of what was to come, except, that is, for another opportunity to fill my stomach.

Having seized the moment later that day, I was sitting in the weather station restaurant willing my body to accept another slice of apple pie and gazing at the collection of stickers on the walls representing a museum and roll of honour for those expeditions which had gone before us. It would have been wrong and a temptation to the Gods of Fate to place ours there before the Pole was ours, but I felt an inner pride at being worthy of a place on a restaurant wall that must only be seen by a few dozen people each year.

After filling our flasks and bidding farewells to Elaine and Shirley, we started out on to the ice, and after a few photographs (camera out again, Mitch) set off for the Pole. The sun was shining and the temperature was -40°C.

On that afternoon, as we left Eureka, we were to be given the first of many lessons on the Arctic. Starting out to cross Eureka Sound and looking into the distance at our route ahead we could see, at what appeared to be about an hour's march, a prominent spur jutting out from an island. We all wanted to camp round this first "corner" on our first night in order to be out of sight of Eureka and the distractions of comfort. Almost four hours later, despite a good pace, we finally reached it and made camp. In the snow and ice-covered wilderness there are no terms of reference upon which the eye can work, nothing by which one can judge distance accurately.

As we were to learn, one must look at the map in order to estimate the most likely time to reach a particular feature. There is nothing quite so morale sapping as to believe the mountain you are heading for to be obtainable by lunch-time and finding that when you make camp at night that you have only covered half the distance. The same illusion of distance applies to size. As we were to discover when we thought the polar bear raiding our sledges was a young cub.

Tonight we made our first contact with the team. It had been awful leaving them at Eureka (in the middle of nowhere), wondering what they might face in the days and weeks to come. The cold here is biting. Walking a few hundred yards from one building to another is enough to take your breath away and cause a burning frost nip to any exposed skin. How would our team survive out there with no solid shelter? It was such a relief to hear Kim's voice coming in loud and clear over the radio. We could have been speaking over the telephone!

Our radio is operated in the Ken Borek Pilot House, where it is sited above a big old freezer. I lean on the freezer during the broadcast, occasionally I forget myself and lean too hard, causing the metal to dint with a loud noise. Standing there tonight, in that warm kitchen with the pilots washing the dinner dishes behind me, I tried to imagine the scene at the receiving end of my transmission. They have made it through one day out there in this bitter weather and they seem to be in good spirits. I hope they continue to be so.

DAY 2 – Monday 6th April

I woke at 6.00 a.m. and it was still blowing a hooley outside. I dozed in my maggot. Normally if it's windy, I would just sleep until the wind subsided. However, we had very limited resources. To reduce the weight, we had kept it to fifteen days' supply and five days' emergency food. This was to cover the two hundred and sixty miles to the Pole.

Reducing our average mileage per day and carrying more food would make the sledges heavier, which would slow us down, hence we would need still more food. What we had was the optimum weight over this distance. If we lost a day, it would put us fifteen miles down, which would mean we would have to make up these miles on the following days.

Next door they were rummaging around, getting breakfast on. This really was the height of luxury. I normally had to cook the food myself and made a pig's ear of it. Hugh put his weather anometer and thermometer outside the door. Wind-chill -55°C – cold enough to give you frostbite in seconds. Breaking camp and loading sledges would be positively dangerous.

Although we had camped with two separate tents, we rigged the doors together. This enabled us to hand food and drink to each other below the door, and talk easily.

After hot oats and tea, Hugh asked what I wanted to do.

"Make the flasks up, give it an hour, and then we'll decide."

One hour later, the tent was still rattling with the wind.

"OK, this is the deal," I said. "We can stop here and sit on our asses, but this storm could last five days, which would mean the end of the expedition if we stayed put. I suggest we get out, try it for one hour, and then decide whether or not to carry on for the day.

"Pack everything up before we get out of the tent. Leave one tent up until the last minute, just in case someone has problems. All of us will take down the tents, so they don't blow down, and watch each other for white patches."

We all crawled out, and within thirty minutes we had broken camp. Quite amazing.

Fortunately, the wind was into our backs, so with a Sprayway wind-proof outer jacket, I was as snug as a bug in a rug. We set off in single file and, after half an hour, everybody was again taking clothes off to cool down – in -55°C! I eventually got down to one thermal layer, with a windproof layer over the top. Without the wind, it would have been glorious. It was quite a strange sensation, as we had beautiful blue skies again, but the wind ripped ruthlessly across the ground taking spindrift with it. Six inches above the ground was like a river of snow; above your knees it was clear, just wind. You couldn't see your boots, and couldn't see where you were putting your feet.

We did marvellously well, actually walking for seven hours, keeping the hourly stops to a minimum so as not to get cold. We had covered a good twelve to thirteen miles without any problems.

By this time we were again near to land. I talked to the lads as we walked. "Hugh will choose a camp site. Listen to his instructions, but basically do everything in reverse from this morning."

All of us pitched in to quickly erect one tent and get dug in. Then up with the next tent. Again we each had our allotted tasks, and naturally we all complained bitterly that our own task was the hardest. I had to roll the dipoles out, being careful not to snag them or snap them.

The wind was still blowing hard, with a wind-chill now of -60°C. Next to land we came across wolf droppings and during the night we heard a loud cry from the hills. Jock was paranoid about polar bears, and made sure the rifle was close at hand.

I got into my maggot aching and hurting just about everywhere. It crossed my mind that I was getting too old for this boy scout lark. Mitch suffered that day too, already I thought he was feeling dizzy from the lack of food. He scoffed the evening meal down, to the customary chorus of "I could eat that again." I suppose it was nice for Hugh to be appreciated as a cook, but not so nice when everyone complained, through no fault of your own, that they were starving.

The radio sked with Elaine was poor. We could hardly hear her, but we managed to take down the Argos latitude and longitude and she told us it would be windy again tomorrow. As we were getting good Argos positions, we kept the Trimble and Magellan well wrapped up for future use in case the Argos wasn't working. Also, I was anxious to prevent their liquid displays from freezing.

The whole team, especially Neill and Jock, had performed tremendously so far. The Arctic is such a surreal place. A place of contrasts. On the one hand, cold, sterile and harsh, yet at the same time warm, friendly and inviting. It would be so easy to forget how dangerous it is. How unforgiving to those who drop their guard for a single instance.

I wondered how we would have got on had we had parachutes to pull us. We probably would have doubled our distance. I went to sleep thinking of a meal at Le Suchet. A huge bowl of mussels with French bread, followed by a seafood platter. I could even taste the wine. I was like Pavlov's dog. My stomach was aching for food.

DAY 2 – Mitch's Journal

Dawn on the first morning set us off on a routine that was to last for the next nineteen days: melt snow for water, cook breakfast, fill the flasks to keep the fluid intake going for the day, break the ice which forms round the opening of one's sleeping bag, put on our boots, climb out into the cold outside air, collapse the tents, pack the sledges and set off for the Pole.

For the next three weeks we were to transform ourselves into walking machines. If we were not in the tents refuelling our bodies with food and sleep, we were on the ice heading for the Pole. The beauty and splendour of the terrain was soon taken for granted and by day three the main problem (for me at least) was one of intense boredom and a need to keep my thoughts occupied. I tried in vain, using a variety of methods ranging from counting right then left steps alternately; to making mental pictures of the patterns in the ice and singing songs in my mind. By the end of the journey I could make a "Rolo" last seven minutes (or 527 steps) and a chunk of "Yorkie" a massive eighteen minutes. In order to cover the ground as efficiently as possible we adopted a single file march, the lead man breaking the trail and flattening any snow, making it easier for those following in his sledge tracks. Subsequently, conversation was reduced to zero and each team member was left to his own thoughts for up to ten hours a day. We marched for between one and one and a half hours at a time, with five minute breaks to snatch a hot drink, check headings and change the lead man. These stops were not always welcome as there was nowhere to shelter from the wind. Without the effort of walking with one hundred and fifty pounds of sledge to slow you down, the body very quickly begins to cool. During the day we ate from what became affectionately known as "monster bags" – a plastic bag with the day's ration comprising a broken mixture of chocolate, raisins, peanuts and biscuits. Although we were on 5500 calories a day (courtesy of the Army Arctic ration pack), we nevertheless all felt permanently hungry. By the end of the expedition nobody lost less than twenty pounds.

Camp was dropped quickly today and with the wind in our backs we set off. Initially the pace was very quick to warm us up, but slowed to an easier rate when this desired effect was achieved.

Jock led. Due to wind-chill the breaks were of short duration. The going was good and flat and although all our glasses are steaming, the views are amazing. Today we spotted animal droppings – dog, or fox maybe?

Today's camp site is on the left of the route. Camp went up very quickly, team working well and radio contact established. The night was very cold due to slight dampness.

DAY 3 – Tuesday 7th April

Once again, the wind tugging on the tent awoke me. Life with my daughter Alicia had taught me to cat nap in between her jumping on my head, and doing jigsaws on the bed, or to fitfully doze through screaming habdabs because she had lost her teddy bear under the duvet. Now I was trying to sleep between gusts of wind, Mitch snoring and talking in his sleep, and Jock waking everyone intermittently because he couldn't sleep. He was having problems with his sleeping bag.

On a previous expedition I had learned the hard way that cooking meals inside your tent gives you carbon monoxide poisoning and causes condensation in your sleeping bag. I had good cause to be particularly sensitive to this. There had been an occasion when Steve Vincent and myself were sleeping in the base hut at Eureka on the

Geographical Pole expedition. I was in one room occupying the top bunk. Steve was next door on the bottom bunk in a nice heated room. I had awoken one morning with a splitting headache and feeling sick. Shouting to Steve to get the breakfast on, I heard no reply. I tried to move, but felt extremely lethargic. Eventually, I managed to roll off the top bunk crashing heavily on to the floor. Crawling into Steve's room, I found him lying there, blue in the face. Picking him up in my arms, and shuffling on my knees, I threw him out the back door down the steps to get him into the fresh air. That was my first experience of carbon monoxide poisoning. Had we not had bottled oxygen available, he would have died.

For reasons unknown to me, Hugh didn't take my advice concerning carbon monoxide poisoning. He cooked with the doors closed until one day after breakfast he said we had a major problem. "We need an airlift of sleeping bags, because Jock's bag is wet and he can't sleep in the cold."

They had heated the tent until his bag was usable, but we would run out of fuel if we did this each day.

I asked Mitch what he thought. He immediately said it would be a supported trip if we asked for a drop. It was a hard one. Jock would never last if he was losing sleep because he was getting cold. It was time for a conference. We were all sitting up and talking, and although we had separate tents, it was as if we were around a table.

I started off. Although calling in a 'plane would make the trip supported, I had absolutely no objections if safety was an issue. On the other hand, Jock had a second sleeping bag, and his Goretex and Thinsulate thermals could keep him warm to -40°C without a bag. I knew this was so, because I had to sleep in just these before when I had exactly the same problem. I had cooked in the tent on my

Geographical Pole expedition. Mitch had two parkas, so he could give one to Jock, and the temperatures should warm up to -20°C. Also, as we got further into the trip, we would become more acclimatised. We would play it day by day. Neill said he wished he could get as "little" sleep as Jock. If Jock's snoring was anything to go by, he wasn't doing too badly!

As it registered -55°C wind-chill again that day, we broke camp, using the same routine as the day before. Through eyelids clamped down against the wind, we could only just see our destination, Depot Point. It looked ten minutes away. Jock took the lead. He was proving quite skilled at setting the pace, and enjoyed being out in front. The scenery was opening up. It was quite stunning in every direction. We could see musk oxen on the shore. How these animals survive in this unrelenting climate is beyond belief. They look like shaggy Aberdeen Angus, but I am sure if you shaved them, you would probably just have an animal the size of a greyhound.

Four hours on, and we gradually crept past Depot Point. Distances were so deceiving. We thought we would reach the Point the previous night, but were well adrift in our estimation.

Our next stop would be lunch. Lunch in reality was an extra five minutes to our usual stopping-time, and an extra munch from the Monster Bag, a pre-weighed polythene bag of goodies such as chocolate squares, Rolos, peanuts, biscuits and dextrose tablets for glucose. This enabled us to keep our calorie intake up while we were walking.

We headed towards a huge iceberg. It was still blowing a strong gale, so we all huddled on the leeward side of the iceberg, out of the wind. It was the first opportunity we had had that day to relax.

Out of the biting wind it was beautiful. Mitch dove straight into his paulk, and legged off with a toilet roll. Two minutes later he was back. The very thought started my bowel muscles to have contortions. I had learned to take plenty of fluids and be regular each day to avoid constipation. The thought of baring my backside in -60°C was off-putting. Yielding to the inevitable, I toddled off. From my previous Arctic experience I had a set routine. Scrape a hole, undo the clips on my salopettes, ensuring my braces wouldn't flap around in anything, take a whizz first and empty my bladder. Only then, drop my thermals and do the biz. I had learned from bitter experience, take your gloves off when wiping your bum. Straight up with the thermals. Warm your hands up, then get dressed again, followed by covering everything. Man is quite strange, well this man is. On my solo trips, for some strange reason, even though I knew nobody was around for hundreds of miles, I would still look around to see if anyone was watching.

Lunch over we headed off again. The afterglow when you have emptied your bowels following three days' abstention is quite fantastic. I knew then, my body wouldn't allow me that luxury again. On a diet of peanuts, I would become as regular as Big Ben.

The next hour, it was Jock's turn. He scurried away. We had even brought a seat for him to sit on. It was a fishing stool with a hole in it, referred to as his "portable crapper". Everyone was joking the first five minutes. After ten minutes standing around, it was getting cold. After fifteen minutes, we were getting seriously cold. We endured another five minutes of his barracking. This had to stop. It would be tragic to get frostbite because someone took too long over a dump. It was agreed, if we could, we would have a dump first thing in the morning or night. If things got desperate on the road, the others would walk one quarter speed just to keep warm.

Everyone had their own methods, but Mitch broke all records for completing the task in the minimal amount of time. He put it down to the fact he had been deep in the "oh nasty" all his life.

Hugh found a campsite in the middle of the Sound. The Sawtooth Mountain Range was in the distance. Aptly named, its mountains form an outline that strikingly resemble a sawtooth. We had done a brilliant day's walk, considering the conditions, but we had now fallen about a day's march behind. Hugh had us in our tents and food in our stomachs within an hour. We warmed the radio batteries up next to the stove. Elaine came in loud and clear. "British Mobile, British Mobile," booming around the tent. It really does lift your spirits to know you are not forgotten by the civilised world. She first gave us the Argos position, then the weather forecast which predicted thirty kilometre winds for the next day. This was strange as the wind had died away and it was lovely inside the tent.

I dozed off thinking of steak and kidney pie and chips with baked beans. Luckily we had forsworn having baked beans. Basic tent rules included no belching or other windward activities. I think Mitch cheated on one or two of these rules. I could hear Jock snoring next door. At least he was getting some sleep. He's a hard nut.

Day 3 – Hugh's Journal

Last night was very cold and I am concerned about the sleeping bags due to ice forming between the bags and the bivi. Have had to cut the lining out of Pertex, as water freezes between layers, also Pertex seems to be less breathable. It is very cold and the wind chill is dangerous. The day's march was excellent but distances are difficult to judge. An estimated march of three hours can turn out to be a day's hard slog. I find the pace slow but at the end of the day Neill was feeling dizzy so we camped short of land. The snow is deep, making it hard going, but pitching the tent is easy.

Today the temperature is good. Rose to -25°C but by nightfall to -30°C. Sleeping bags are now a cause for concern, Jock's outer is damp, making him cool down at night. Tomorrow we will have to attempt to dry it! Otherwise we are in good spirits and looking forward to the completion of the expedition.

Tried to tell base our location.

"We are at Depot."

"What?"

"We are at Depot."

"What?"

"Forget it!"

Day 3 – Neill's Journal

The wind was far too strong to break camp until 11.00 a.m. but we still managed six and a half hours' walking. Soft snow cover makes walking difficult and I make lots of mistakes. We all dehydrate and I suffer more than the rest of the team. Buddy buddy systems save us from serious problems and Hugh's general cheerfulness keeps you on your toes. The radio works well and informs us that the weather is going to get colder. It can't get colder – the bottom will fall out of the thermometer! All our sleeping bags are getting damp and I feel miserable and dejected when I crawl into mine. I am able to get warm and go to sleep, but wake up cold. The worst experience so far is putting your head out of the sleeping bag for the first time in the morning. I must now eat and drink everything offered to keep my body balance correct.

Day 3 – Elaine May's Journal

Today the team was moving down the channel and making little progress. Each morning Bezal comes over to the complex with the Argos reading for our team, which he receives daily on his computer. I then sit at the table to plot the previous day's progress, usually with a couple of pilots who are not flying that day looking over my shoulder and offering advice. Yesterday, they made only eight miles! So far the team's progress has been much slower than expected, yet this is supposed to be the easiest part of the trip! If they don't make better time, they will never make it before supplies run out. I would like to ask them about this on the next radio sked, but do not want to dampen their spirits. We'll just have to wait and see.

DAY 4 – Wednesday 8th April

We were up late today – 11.30 a.m. I was a little grumpy because Hugh and Neill were taking so long to do the brews – despite the fact that Hugh had been up late last night preparing them, claiming it would be "quicker" this way.

Late mornings were a loss of valuable time. Although the sun was above the horizon twenty-four hours a day, there was still a definite day and night temperature. We found if we walked until 7.00 or 8.00

p.m., it grew progressively colder, so optimum use could be made of the day if we tried to break camp and get going by 9.00 a.m. We could then walk seven to eight hours at a good pace and make camp in the late afternoon while it was still relatively warm. That gave us plenty of time to sort out the radio sked, flasks, diaries, etc.

Neill crawled out rubbing his eyes. I told Hugh once again I thought it unwise to cook with the door closed, but he felt he had control of the situation. Mitch thought if he killed someone from carbon monoxide poisoning he might change his mind. Jock's sleeping bag was now like a wet lettuce and the thought of a resupply was in the back of my mind.

As it happened, we were on the flight path into Eureka, and there would be no problem in kicking out a bag from a Twin Otter. It was two days before a resupply flight would be a major detour from the 'plane's regular route. Perhaps I was growing older and wiser, I felt the principle was at stake, but my first priority was the safety of my team.

In 1983, during my solo Geographical North Pole expedition, I was out on the polar pack ice when my radio failed. I had lost all communications with the outside world. This was a serious situation and, psychologically, I was in a turmoil. Should I go on or not? If I did I couldn't receive my positions, and my team wouldn't know how I was. Mac and Steve came in to do a resupply, but the radio was shot. Mac thought the best course of action was to go back to our base at Eureka, identify the problem, and rectify it so it wouldn't happen again.

When the radio was repaired I was delivered back to the spot where the aircraft had picked me up. I was criticised, of course, for not starting from scratch again, but at the time the logic of the argument was lost on me. I reasoned that if you get a puncture in a Formula One race, you don't start from lap 1 again, you just carry on from where you finished. Nearly ten years on, I now finally agree with that argument, to the extent that if we did call a 'plane in, we should even consider packing in the expedition.

Neill put my mind at rest when he said he wished he could sleep as much as Jock, and that Jock was as warm as toast. Jock was an experienced sailor, and had been pushed to the limits on more than one occasion and revelled in it. He was again first in line, leading out into the wind. We were making fairly good progress, but slowly falling behind our overall schedule. Jock had the capability of getting in the front and just pushing all day long.

Mitch got out of the tent with his sunglasses on, and started singing the signature tune from the Blues Brothers film which was to become the team National Anthem. Within two minutes, five grown men were pretending to blow saxophones, jigging around putting kit into the sledge. We were always full of beans to get started.

The scenery was strikingly beautiful as we walked towards the Sawtooth Mountains. For the first time in the -40°C air, we could see the yellow tinge of smog from Siberia. What a tragic shame. If only people could see this, the last bastions of wilderness being polluted.

We stopped for a flask of coffee on the hour, and Mitch said that he had spotted two polar bears on the coast. Jock immediately upped the pace. It was as if we were in a rowing boat together. Jock was stroke, so he usually set the pace, until someone else took the lead. But today we all shot down the fjord. Each time we stopped Mitch would nonchalantly say, "Oh yes, they popped over that ridge," and Jock would shoot off again. The Sawtooth Mountains were still in the distance. We nicknamed them "The Frigging Far Away Mountains."

The team was now working well individually and as a team. Everyone complemented each other wonderfully. Neill, shy and retiring, Jock, bold and assertive, Hugh, confident, Mitch, unassuming and strong, and me, just trying to hold the whole thing together.

I changed the lead towards the end of the day as a couple of the team were getting tired. It had been a long day and hard work coping with the wind.

It is often the case that when you push too hard you get injuries at the end of a run. I felt we were still becoming acclimatised, and we should only gradually increase our mileage. Nevertheless, we had done a good day of fifteen miles, and were in the shadow of the Sawtooth. Hugh worked magic with his curry powder and dehydrated goulash, to be rewarded with the usual ring of "I could eat that again."

The radio sked went well, but Elaine said the latest ice thermograph showed the ice bridge starting to eat its way North. The weather station thought if we made good progress we should be OK. It was another turn of the screw of pressure on us to make good time. We were gradually slipping behind, Jock was cold, and we were all now starving. Mitch mentioned fish and chips and two pints of Stella in the Pheasant again. If only we could get a pill to taste like pints of lager.

Jock had forgotten all about the cold. "David, have you got the rifle handy?"

"I haven't got the rifle. Neill, you had it."

"No, Hugh had it."

Jock's jovial Scottish accent had now turned sober. "I'm being serious. If polar bears are around, keep it handy."

Neill was a little homesick today, talking about the boys as we walked side by side. I hoped he was enjoying himself. He was growing in stature every day.

Each man had his forte and his responsibility to the expedition, whilst I fumbled about trying to lead these magnificent men. Hugh wanted to prepare the best meal in the Arctic, Jock wanted to get over the best press release, Neill tried to put the tent up faster each night, and Mitch tried to pull more weight on less calories.

Day 4 – Hugh's Journal

TEMP	-30°C
WIND	10 m.p.h.
CHILL	-43°C
WEATHER	Bright clear day with light winds.

Unfortunately, reports from base suggest -40°C with thirty miles per hour winds. Not so good.

Very cold this morning, I missed the alarm. Jock awoke at 7.00 a.m. and I took thirty minutes to surface. Once the cooker was on it was a different matter. Today I was introduced to the "HEMPLEMAN HAT" (a Flectalon bag) which keeps my head warm. More water consumed than yesterday. Hopefully no more problem.

Jock has a very serious problem with his sleeping bags, both of which are now completely wet. He is not able to sleep at all. All the bags are suffering similarly and are affecting the amount of rest we are getting. Otherwise spirits are high. Food is good and Mulligatawny soup with Tabasco is "the biz".

DAY 5 – Thursday 9th April

Jock was having problems with the inner of his two bags now, but he seemed to be still strong and sleeping well. In fact, he was sleeping better than all of us put together. How the hell his wife sleeps with the noise of his snoring, I'll never know.

It was a beautiful clear day, blue skies and -25°C with no wind. Really quite warm. We could feel the warmth from the sun all over our bodies.

There were now problems with dismantling the tents. We changed the poles from fibreglass to aluminium, but the male and female parts of the joints were freezing together. It took two of us with lighters trying to heat the joints and pull them apart. We didn't actually take the poles out of the tent, we just folded the tents in a way that we could quickly put the joints together again without any fiddling. We had now reduced the time down to two minutes. We then piled snow and ice on the valence to keep the wind from blowing under the tent.

The Sawtooth Mountains were gradually drawing closer. It's really wonderful walking between these beautiful mountains, some of which are still virgin and unclimbed. Quite a contrast to the Alps which are so overrun now. It must be fantastic coming through these fjords in a resupply ship, piling through open water amongst huge icebergs.

Jock was again out in front. I was now trying to keep him in front for periods of four hours, and then alternate the rest of the day with the rest of the team.

I hated it out in front, and the others hated to have me there. I either walked too fast or too slow, never quite the right speed. Mitch sets a good steady pace, which is good towards the end of the day, and Neill's speed had to be regulated by the second man in the line, as he had not learned the difference between fast and a little faster. Instead of going one notch up in speed, he went from fast to ballistic, with me swearing all the way. Hugh was good for the very last hour, setting a good pace at the end of the day.

Mitch walked with me for over an hour that day. He was a little worried about the food. We were five days out and already one third into our food, with well under one fourth of the route covered. He had quickly worked out we would run out even with our emergency food. He said he didn't mind going with less food, but he wasn't going to go without any food.

With that, a ten knot wind, which really hurt, started blowing straight into our faces. Things were going to get tight. The rest of the day I mulled over possible distances we could cover each day and what amount of food would be needed for each scenario. I talked to Hugh and asked him to do an actual food stock-take, to start cutting meals by one tenth, and to save coffee and tea bags for a later time. We had ample fuel. In fact, we had a fifty per cent overkill, so if it really came to it, Jock could still get warm or we could even cook him if need be.

We did a super eight hours walking, which was probably our best run to date, even though we were togged up so no flesh showed. At least a sixteen nautical mile day. In the last hour I promised Jock a meal at the Roux Brothers Restaurant at Bray for doing five days. Psychologically, it was a very important day for Jock and Neill. Now they knew themselves they could work and survive in the lowest of temperatures. I told them at the start, if they could do five days, then they would finish the trip.

Everyone was knackered that night, probably because it was a long day, and we were walking into the wind for the first time. I crawled into my maggot with every bone in my body aching. In fact, I could quite easily have gone to sleep without eating. Inside the tents we were as warm as toast. We had seen a lot of pollution again that day. I hoped the world conference in Rio would get to grips with this problem. Jock seemed to be OK with his maggot at the moment. Hopefully the ambient temperature would climb a little more, although on the radio sked with Elaine that night, we were told the ice bridge on the thermograph was definitely creeping North. This was starting to worry me, because we were still at least ten to twelve days from the Kane Basin. A lot could happen in that time.

Mitch told Jock that polar bears had rabies, and asked him if he wanted some of his serum left over from the Gulf War. I told Jock the story about a pilot who saw a polar bear swimming ten miles out from land, just to get an explorer supper. Ten minutes later he was checking that the rifle was in place again. Mitch and I always kept the door of the inner tent open and the zip half closed, so we could get out quickly if a bear was about. It wouldn't be smart to be stuck in the inner tent.

Settling down to sleep I began my usual routine. I wriggled my feet to the bottom of my bag, and pulled my Mukluk boots inside the door. I then took out their linings and put them into my sleeping bag to try and dry out. I took the felts out and put them down my front, and kept the wire meshing in the boot overnight just in case I had to get out. I would shake them free of frozen sweat first thing in the morning. I wear two pairs of thermal Damart socks, and change the inners and outers over each night, keeping my nails short if I can. I then put them into a Flectalon bag, made out of strips of fine aluminium which reflect body heat. Neill and Hugh found them useful as head-warmers. I wriggled my feet into the Flectalon bag, in turn into the first bag, and then into the second. I pulled everything up past my bum, checked my pillow (consisting of my parka) for the last time, checked that the insulation mats were in place; and checked that the gloves and socks I had been wearing during the day were inside my armpits drying out. I also made sure the radio batteries were inside the sleeping bag. This done I pulled the first bag over my shoulders, then the second. A mammoth task then ensued to arrange the balaclava over my nose while I slept. The next task involved pulling the cords on the bag to bring the hood close to my head, so that just my eyes and mouth were open to the elements within the tent – again I took care not to fully tie the cord, so I could get out easily if need be in an emergency. Finally, I always kissed a photograph of Alicia and Claire.

When I was snug and settled and about to go to sleep, Mitch would always start his lecturing. I have known Mitch for a long time now, and when he's tired he has a habit of giving me a lecture on anything that comes to his mind: how fast I should walk, how untidy I am, what a slob I am, etc. I usually nod and doze off, unless I have to jab him with an elbow to get him to be quiet.

I shouted out to Jock and Neill to congratulate them for completing the fifth day and becoming true Arctic explorers. They had performed magnificently. I dozed off, thinking of that meal I was going to treat Jock to. Lovely fish, wine, and coffee on the terrace, overlooking the Thames.

Jock woke Hugh and I early. We had a major problem – he was freezing cold and had to get into Hugh's bag for some sleep (Hugh got out first!). As soon as breakfast was over Hugh started the spare stove and, after tying Jock's inner bag to the centre of the tent, we ended up sitting in a sauna, stripped to our pants, attempting to break up the sodden down in Jock's bag.

Rest of the day was a downer. We all plodded along and for the first time Hugh was not on top of things. I'm experiencing something here unique to me. Outside of family, no one has looked out for me in this way, nor have I had the responsibility for their well-being.

Sleep was not pleasant, feet got cold again and I feel very claustrophobic in my bag. There is always something to moan about if you want. I suppose the long periods walking in line make your mind concentrate and exaggerate the aches and pains. Wonder what the children are doing.

CHAPTER SIX

STRANGERS IN THE NIGHT

DAY 6 – Friday 10th April

Since it was constant daylight and we were all getting tired, we needed someone to wake the rest of us up – we volunteered Neill. Hugh, Neill and Jock then took turns preparing the breakfast.

While Mitch and I floated between fits of dozing and grappled with the thought of getting out of our bags, we could hear the stove blast into life. Its wild roar brought warmth to our insides as we knew hot grub would soon be wanging through the door. We then dozed until we had a ten minute warning from the next tent that the flasks would soon be ready. At that, Mitch and I would grovel out of the bag, slowly and deliberately change our socks around again, pull our thermals and Mukluk liners on, put the wire mesh into the boot, then lace up the Mukluks. We then put on our outer jackets and gloves and crawled out.

This morning was different. My toe nail had been playing up the whole of yesterday, so I decided to have breakfast in the warm tent, and let Hugh look at my toe. It was like the Bahamas in there and I offered to paint palm trees on the sides of the tent. Within two minutes I was too hot, and began frantically trying to get clothes off so I wouldn't sweat. Jock was still asleep, dead to the world.

I had an inflamed ingrown toe nail. Quite an innocuous injury, but

111

it hurt like hell. The problem was we only had a pair of crummy little plastic first aid scissors. As these proved totally inadequate, the only thing I could do was use a Swiss Army knife to cut it out. Amazing the number of volunteers I had to do it. They all wanted to inflict some pain on me for getting them into this.

It was lovely to get back into the cold tent. I told Mitch to go next door for a sauna, and back into our tent for the cold plunge pool.

I crawled out. It was -32°C with no wind. We were right under the Sawtooth Mountains. You could really feel the warmth on your body. Absence of wind makes such a difference.

Our tent came down first, and our paulks were usually packed before the hot tent came down. Mitch now realised that if he started off with the Blues Brothers tune, it would set us off in a good mood. For his finale he would break into the Birdie Song, which I hated, but would nevertheless find myself humming all day. Each morning we would slip into our respective tasks. While the hot tent was being packed, I would roll up the radio dipoles and sort the skis out. Mitch would sort the monster bags, only because he could choose the biggest. Meanwhile, Jock would struggle putting all of his kit into his sledge.

Having checked everyone was ready, I would get the map out and give a quick brief of the route. Mitch would always check my neck was covered by my scarf. Then away, Jock leading out. Each day I would try and advise, but never insist on doing anything. With Jock, each day I tried to get him to do the first hour slowly. As before, we found we would race for an hour, then be knocked out for the rest of the day.

Slowly we made our way to the edge of the mountain and into Vessel Fjord, which was due East for us and a change of direction. We had bet each other a pint it would only take two hours to get into the bay. As usual we had been totally deceived by the apparent distance. In fact we took double our estimated time. Within a short space of time we came across a number of bear prints, plus wolf and fox droppings. We were impressed with the size of the prints, they were huge. This was definitely the Daddy bear. Jock felt a sudden urge to check the rifle, and shot off like a bullet.

We were looking for an island called Lois Island which had a five hundred foot contour. Within sight was a huge island that looked well over a thousand feet. Could that be it? Mitch insisted it was. I told him the tax payers' contribution to the education budget had been wasted if he thought that was Lois Island. We bet each other another pint of Stella. He now had a lead of forty-two to my thirty-five pints. It was becoming an expensive trip!

In this strange environment it is easy for the eye to be deceived. For some reason when you are slogging along in your own dream world, the horizon always looks as if you are skiing uphill, and if you look back, it always looks as if you have skied downhill. Quite bizarre.

At 7.30 p.m. we stopped and put the tents up. I made it a practice to be last in, having checked everything was secure, while the lads next door quickly got into action with the food.

My sledge did duty as a bear decoy. With a quantity of food placed on top, it was sited approximately fifty feet away, in line with the door flap. The area reminded me of Polar Bear Pass on Bathurst and I decided to keep the rifle close by.

We had a good radio sked with Elaine. Jock was able to communicate in his broad Scottish accent. "We are now in Vessel Bay, V for vehicle, E for envelope, S for Strathclyde, S for Stansted, E for eiderdown, L for lunatic." Knowing Jock to be very familiar with the phonetic alphabet, I suspected he was winding up our listeners in the Arctic, including Hugh. Jock had joined the expedition with the specific assignment of undertaking the PR function. Matching Neill and Mitch in determination to prove their professionalism and dedication, he insisted on getting out his PR copy to Elaine. If need be, he would try and try again until he had done it, often well after everyone else had gone to sleep. That night Elaine informed us that the Conservatives had won the election. More tea was ordered to celebrate.

Elaine then read a fax from Yvonne to Hugh saying how much she loved him and missed him. I was totally against this. It made the individual receiving the message homesick, and made the rest of us wonder why we hadn't heard anything ourselves.

I was well asleep when I heard, "David, David, quick. Something's outside." I grabbed the rifle, screaming and shouting, and looked outside the tent. To my amazement, a polar bear was sitting fifty feet away watching us. It had sniffed the sledge, walked through our camp, sniffed at Jock's head and walked past. I didn't know what to do.

I knew it could come back and stalk us, but I was given such a hard time the last time I killed a bear I didn't want to do it again unless absolutely necessary.

"Mitch, if we have to kill it, will you do it?"

The bear looked at us pensively. I fired a warning shot over its behind. It turned, and, as if to put two fingers up to us, walked slowly away. I tracked it for fifteen minutes, then got back in the tent.

Ten minutes later, to put my mind at rest, I double checked to see if our visitor had decided to return, and blow me, there was another bear tracking along the coast. This really must be polar bear country. Jock thought we should post a guard, and take it in turns to keep watch. But we were so knocked out and in need of sleep, within two minutes of the suggestion we had all crashed out. I dreamt of polar bear steaks with chips.

Day 6 – Mitch's Journal

On the morning of day six we were to encounter what was to be a most serious problem. At 2.30 a.m. I was awoken to a question from Neill in the other tent, who was wondering what one of us was doing wandering about outside! Since both of us sharing the second tent were firmly ensconced in our sleeping bags I assumed him to have been dreaming and told him so. By the time he had confirmed that his three crew were similarly disposed we quickly put two and two together and realised something was outside! Kim – whose previous experience in the Arctic has given him paranoia about becoming a tent-wrapped pre-packed polar bear lunch – wasted no time in exiting his sleeping bag, grabbing the ever ready rifle and throwing open the tent. In what must have taken over sixty seconds, during which time much shouting and commotion took place, whatever it was that was disturbing our camp site took fright. I remained in my sleeping bag as we looked out of the tent. We saw a polar bear making for the hills. Kim's past experience inclined him to shoot, as he knew these animals had been known to track parties such as ours and attack at night. With poor eyesight they have no fear of man, assuming us to be vertical seals – or so we were informed by one of the Innuit hunters at Resolute Bay. Looking at the bear I estimated it to be a small cub and advised against shooting it, both on humanitarian grounds and the fact that all killings have to be reported to the Royal Canadian Mounted Police (RCMP) for registration and other lengthy procedures, which would have used up our precious time. As an alternative, Kim fired a warning shot to hurry its escape. After a couple of photographs we returned to our sleeping bags. It was only on inspecting the footprints the following morning, that we realised the previous lesson, relating to the problem of estimating size and distance in this strange environment, had been ignored! I was wearing size twelve Mukluks and the bear's pug was larger than my footprint!

Day 6 – Neill's Journal

Couldn't get to sleep last night despite being very tired. Camped in the heart of polar bear country and guess what visited the camp – a foraging polar bear. In the early hours of the morning, I heard something outside which came close to the tent within a few feet of our heads. I chose to do nothing, thinking it would sniff around and leave. It would be difficult to get out of my sleeping bag without disturbing the others and who knows what would have happened in the ensuing confusion should the bear be an adult male! Jock was also awake, his reaction was to alert Kim, who grabbed the rifle and left the tent. This sudden movement made the bear turn and take another look at us. Kim fired a shot above its head to make sure that it would not return.

Walked for the first part of the day before putting skis on. I had not been on skis since I was eighteen and I thoroughly enjoyed the experience.

We did nine hours, some of it uphill, with the result that we are all bushed. It is now fairly certain that this will take longer than we thought – well, we will see!

Poor sleep again, feeling very damp and claustrophobic in the sleeping bags. Poor Jock is in a mess. I don't envy his sleeping arrangements. However, he remains in good spirits. We have all given him kit to make sure he keeps warm.

Kim and Mitch are funny. They are great friends, and, at times when they are correcting each other, sound like an old married couple.

Day 6 – Jock's Journal

As usual, I was first asleep – I tried to take advantage of what warmth there was in the tent because my bag, even though we had played around with it the previous night, was not in the best of conditions. Once again my hours of sleep were short and perhaps in some ways that was very fortunate as I woke up at about three o'clock in the morning to what sounded like a dog panting outside. As I lay there and tried to convince myself I was dreaming, I heard one of the paulks move and I saw this creature brushing against the tent. I knew then that it was not my imagination and decided that the best thing to do was to get the man with the gun out. I gave a yell – "Kim, there's a polar bear outside." I must say I was quite impressed with the speed of his reactions, as, with very little hesitation, Kim was outside saying, "God, yes, it's a polar bear" and he was obviously very agitated. I was still trying to find my way out of the tent, not wishing to

117

get caught inside with a large animal trying to get at me for supper, when I heard the gun go off as Kim put a bullet over its head. I looked outside to see a rather shaken Kim aiming the rifle at this furry object and Mitch clutching his ears as Kim had fired very close to Mitch's head when Mitch had been trying to get a photograph. On previous expeditions Kim has had a bear coming through the tent trying to eat him. At the same time, Hugh was coming out of a very deep sleep and muttering about "Don't kill the thing, it's only a small one." The combination of Kim's agitation, Hugh's remarks and the sight of Mitch hugging his ears was just too much for me and I started to roll with laughter.

DAY 7 – Saturday 11th April

For the first time in the whole expedition, Jock was first up and out of the tent. "Look at this, look at this, two inches from my head," he yelped, looking down at the bear footprint. One by one we piled out to join him. It was a beautiful day once again. Mitch winked at me, and said to Jock, "This was a baby bear." Mitch then said he had seen two huge bears the size of bulldozers walking along the coast. Jock thought we might skip breakfast and get going. "David, I think we should walk closely together today. I wouldn't mind carrying the rifle."

The weather was getting warmer, the paulks slightly lighter, and each of us more and more confident in ourselves and as a team. It really was a fantastic feeling to be out in the middle of nowhere. Today would be our first land crossing. If the huge mountain in the middle of the fjord was Lois Island, then this would be an ominous omen. Our maps showed no contours over five hundred feet on our crossing, and it looked straightforward on the map. We could be in for a hard day.

We had heard the night before that Jim May, our major sponsor, and his colleagues were due to fly up in seven days time. I was starting to get worried. We were gradually falling behind schedule. We would never make the Pole by the following week and we had the big problem of the Ellesmere crossing still to come.

We started off as normal. Mitch nonchalantly relayed to Jock a polar bear story which he had heard in Resolute. Something about a polar bear tracking an explorer and waiting with his big furry arm over his nose, so he couldn't be seen. Just when the guy saw the bear, that was it!

"That was what?"

"The bear ate him for breakfast."

Ten minutes later, Jock said, "Actually I wouldn't mind someone else taking the lead today!"

For the last couple of days my Achilles tendon had been hurting, an old running injury – why do you always get injuries when you don't need them? Today I could hardly put any weight on it. I tried to walk through the pain, but it was no good. Hugh gave me some pain killers and I took them every four hours. They seemed to do the trick. I just hoped the injury wouldn't slow me and the team down. Neill was quite concerned, Jock said it was sweet justice for letting him get so cold.

We passed Lois Island. It must have been nine hundred and ninety-nine feet and just missed the second contour line. Mitch stopped.

"Well."

"Well what?"

"I was right."

"So?"

"You maligned my navigation yesterday, and you owe me another pint of Stella."

"Sorry, Mitch."

"Sorry, is that all?"

"Hold it."

Everyone stumbled to a halt. We were all spread out over one hundred metres. It was only Mitch and myself walking together.

"Get together." Everyone looked a little concerned. "Yesterday, I made a terrible mistake, I called Mitch's navigation and parenthood into question. I would like to make a public apology that I got the navigation wrong."

"You prat!" Neill said, "I thought something serious had happened."

Although we were getting tired, and a little worried, we were also becoming closer as a team. Each stop, Jock would help Neill. Neill would offer a chocolate to Mitch, who would snatch his hand off. We were all helping each other and bonding together.

We finally came to the top of Vessel Fjord. It was time for climbing over land. We donned our skis. They were so different from the skis I had used the previous year. They were the real McCoy. Mitch led off. Neill was like a Bambi on ice, trying to keep up while pulling his heavy sledge. He gradually got into the swing of things. Our paulks preventing us from making a straight ascent, we climbed and climbed in long sweeping traverses. As we got higher, ranges of mountains unfolded all around us. The sweat and toil had its rewards in the beautiful surroundings.

The skis we had been given from Fischer in Austria, made all the difference. Instead of the old moleskins on the bottoms, a new design of fish scales covering about one foot along the base gave us the traction. They would save us hours, although we seemed still to be climbing up, and not making any true progress. A lot can happen in a five hundred contour, and it was happening to us. What looked like a flat crossing turned out to be a switchback of undulating hills. The only consolation was the scenery.

We camped on a mountain, absolutely exhausted. Hugh wanted to up the calories for us. We were already eating 6000 per day, but we were probably burning up 10,000. I asked Hugh to bulk the food out with left-overs from our monster bags, "But don't use double rations, just in case things get tight."

Although we were a captive audience, Hugh's cooking was just first class. Before we had the main meal, we would tuck into a mug of soup. Mulligatawny with Tabasco really did revive the spirits.

This was the time I would pick up my diary, find a pencil, and jot down some thoughts. I turned to the front of the book and worked out twenty days. Mitch didn't say a word, but sat up and looked at what I was writing. We had already used up seven days' food, slightly over a third of the total amount. However, we had not quite covered a third of the total expedition distance. We were stuck on the side of the mountain, making little progress, and we still had the two potentially difficult parts to tackle, Sverdrup Pass and the Kane Basin. Over two thirds still to go, with less than two thirds of the food remaining, including our emergency food. I marked out days eight through twenty. Hopefully we would make Bay Fjord tomorrow, the top of Irene by day nine. Three days to cross Ellesmere. Mitch raised an eyebrow but didn't say anything. One day to cross the Bach, two days to walk the whole length, which would give us four days for the Basin. Mitch and I stretched the maps out, and plotted our best days. It didn't look tight, it looked impossible! We would have to increase our average, have no problems, and have good weather if we were going to make it.

On top of that, the radio sked was very poor. Jock wanted desperately to tell Elaine about the polar bear, but just couldn't get the story over. The food came through, steaming hot. We both gulped it down. I was still starving. How could I push them any harder? They were all giving one hundred per cent.

Jock was passing the time by taking an inventory of the team. He asked how many "O" levels we had. He eventually worked out that within the team we had five wives, ten "A" levels, forty "O" levels, four degrees and one post graduate degree, and eight and a half kids (Claire was pregnant). Neill asked Hugh if he wanted kids and we all bombarded him with ideas to get his wife pregnant.

"A bottle of champagne first."

"Chinese nosh followed by a foot massage."

"A brick in a washing machine and sit on top."

It was harmless, tension-relieving fun, and an indication of how close a group we were becoming.

I started to doze off. "Hugh, I want to talk about food to you tomorrow," I called.

Mitch said, "So do I. Why can't you make a bloody steak and

kidney pie out of those Arctic rations?"

I tossed and turned all night. I thought of food, and Wally Herbert going through the Sverdrup Canyon. It had taken him nine days just to get through the canyon, let alone the rest of Ellesmere. I was looking at half that time for the whole crossing of Ellesmere, including the Canyon. What was I doing to my lads?

DAY 7 – Shirley Chenoweth's Journal

Had a shower – everything working. Leisurely morning – wrote postcards. Elaine checked weather about 12.30. Terry Jesudason picked us up at 1.45 to go to village, where we had tea and drinks at the Inn (High Arctic) she and Bezal operate. Went over Argos readings. We will transmit to team by radio. They covered better than five miles yesterday, if we're figuring right. Walked over to Co-op – very basic store. Picked up   there by Elaine from Narwhal Inn to go home. Met Lisa who launches balloons from weather station. Greg and Mike fixed fried onions and bacon and macaroni for supper. At 7.00 p.m. Elaine contacted team by radio – couldn't make out anything they said, except that they could hear us, and "roger" and "over and out". Sat around in evening. I had got ready for bed (10.15), when Elaine knocked on my door to say she wanted to tackle the huge pile of big pans and utensils left in the sink from the last two nights. Wanted help, so we did them all – then watched Cheers with Greg, and so to bed to read – Elaine on phone to British radio and TV people in morning.

DAY 8 – Sunday 12th April

Hugh and I emerged from the tents. I wanted to discuss the food in private. I thought it was unwise to tell Jock and Neill. Ignorance was bliss. I quickly went through the route, and our estimated revised schedule. It would be uncomfortably close, even with emergency food. Hugh was, as usual, up-beat. "OK, I'll check the food again. We have plenty of fuel, and I'll start to keep the tea bags for a rainy day."

The weather seemed to be improving all the time. We could see our route in front of us. How easy it would be was another story. It's surprising what a good night's sleep does for you. I asked Hugh to take the lead. I wanted to push the pace a little, to make a start on achieving my revised objectives.

"OK, lads, crux day," I said. "We must get into Bay Fjord by tonight."

We slowly climbed another mountain on skis, then over a scarp and what a beautiful sight! We could see the Bay in front of us, with a frozen river meandering all the way down to the shore. A distance of seemingly two or three miles, so probably a lot further. I switched Neill over to the front. "OK, let's go for the shore, Neill." My Achilles tendon was still playing up and I was taking two tablets every four hours to try and relieve the pain. I hoped nobody else would sustain any injuries, because I was now going through the tablets like Smarties.

The river was all down hill. We came down into the valley, footprints of fox and musk oxen everywhere. How on earth do they survive? A new set of mountains came into view as we hit the fjord. I was relieved. My first objective in the revised plan had been reached. I wanted to push on, although it was getting late. I asked Jock and Mitch to do an hour each in front. My men were performing magnificently, and rising to the occasion. We came across a blow hole later in the day. As soon as I saw it, I wanted to do another hour's walk. If you get seals popping up, there is more than an even chance polar bears will not be far away. Jock didn't need much persuading and off he went again. I was becoming apprehensive. The Ellesmere crossing would soon be upon us. Mitch saw some musk oxen on the shore.

"How about shooting one of those and having a barbecue?" Neill laughed.

"No, seriously . . . "

He was!

"I want a hard push tomorrow, fellas," I told them, "so get some sleep."

When the food came through, Mitch said, "I wonder if it would taste like beef."

"What?"

"Musk oxen."

"Jock," I called, "can you remember that crash in the Andes when the Peruvian rugby players had to eat each other to stay alive?"

"Yes."

"Well Mitch reckons you're the meatiest, so don't die or else. It's going to be a crux day tomorrow."

"You've said that every day."

"Well, I mean it, until we get picked up."

Apple crumble with cream, what I could do with apple crumble – what I could do with anything! Even Neill, who had had to force food down himself in the beginning was now having no problems in eating the lot. Finished was the friendly passing around of chocolate. The only things that got passed around now were the dextrose tablets, which I couldn't stand. Now they were being bartered, the current exchange rate being one Rolo to twenty dextrose.

The sked was poor again. Every expedition in the Arctic seemed to want to talk tonight. Someone had gone through the ice somewhere so I felt they had priority. Mind you, the Spanish base camp leader must have talked for an hour in Spanish to his team. I think he was updating them with the football results. Jock was not pleased. He still wanted to get his bear story out.

Day 8 – Jock's Journal

Hugh, who is an experienced mountaineer, took over in the more mountainous conditions we were now facing. He really is like a mountain goat, extremely strong, and he found for us a frozen river which was like a highway to the sea. Down that for five hours and then I moved into the front again for a couple of hours across the ice trying to keep the pace up. This ability of mine to switch off is a real God-send. One of the things I do think about, and the one vision I have that keeps going through my mind, is reading a story to Gregory in bed and of lifting Laurie up in the morning and, of course, giving my wife a big hug. That certainly seems to sustain me.

DAY 9 – Monday 13th April

I was having terribly restless nights now. Jock had mentioned he had to get back to work on a certain date, or he would lose a large contract. Hugh said he was due to fly out to Belize at the end of the month, and his career would be hindered if he missed the flight. I was wondering if we would make it before Jim May had to go home. Mitch and Neill were homesick, and we didn't seem to be getting any closer to our objective. What I had thought would be a doddle was now starting to turn into a frantic race. But my biggest overall worry was the ice. If we were unlucky, we would hit open water in the Kane Basin.

I was the first out of the tent that day. I began to suspect the lads had also started to become concerned. Jock had said for the last four days, "Right, twenty miles today." We had never once done that distance, but that's what we needed. I decided to tell Jock to start slowly, not to pace out for the first hour. It had become quite obvious when we flew into the day, we were all bushed after six hours. If we paced ourselves slowly throughout the day, we could walk for nine hours and cover a greater distance. The mighty Jock found this hard to believe, but he did what he was told, heading along the coast towards Irene Bay.

Suddenly, Mitch started to yell. A large filling had dropped out. Brilliant. Hugh and I discussed who would re-fill it. I had taken a dentistry course before we came away. Unfortunately, I had only been required to learn to carry out fillings on false teeth. We opened his mouth and asked him to say "Ahh."

"Ahh."

"Louder."

"AHHH."

Hugh said, "I think we're going to have to pull this one out. Who's got the morphine?"

With that Mitch was on his feet. "No way, José! I can tolerate the pain."

Jock was sitting on his sledge sorting out huge blisters, and my Achilles tendon was now needing a stronger pain killer. We were all getting run down, and were not even halfway.

The weather was lovely and warm at -30°C. We passed next to some cliffs with some fantastic patterns in the rocks. I took some snaps for Professor David Dinley, who had given us a tutorial on how they were formed just before we had left. He really brought those pieces of rock to life for us now. We slowly turned into Irene Bay. The scenery changed constantly. One part looked like the Alps, another like Snowdonia and in other places it looked like the Brecons. We were now coming into view of some mountains at the edge of Irene Bay that looked the spitting image of the Grand Tetons in the States. Neill said, "Even if we got picked up today, it's been worthwhile, just for the scenery." We could now see Thumb Mountain, which overlooks the gateway to the Pass of Ellesmere. I had planned and dreamt of seeing that mountain for years. I could hardly believe it. It looked so close, but I had no doubt it was a good day's walk from our present position. It was in this Bay Wally Herbert had received supplies. He had been attempting to reach Eureka surviving only on food from the land. He must have been as worried as I was at that moment, bugged by nagging thoughts that we still had the difficult stage to come.

We camped under the view of those beautiful mountains. It had been a long, hard day, but a satisfactory distance had been covered. Tomorrow we would be on solid land. Hugh started to dig out the site for the tents. I asked him which area he intended pitching our tent. For the past few nights he had been getting cheesed off with Mitch and me pulling back the powder snow cover on to the ice he had just excavated.

"Why did you ask me to be camp administrator, to set up the tents, when you both go and kick the snow back into the hole?"

"It's not all the snow, but every night we have had a snow layer for insulation. I'm not stopping you from camping on the ice."

We all crawled into our tents, drained. Jock was most insistent that we had a good radio sked. He still hadn't got his bear story out.

"Bollocks to the PR," said Hugh.

"Hold on a minute," I said. "You have your duties, and you do them well. Jock just wants to do his duties well, but we're not giving him the opportunity." Things were getting tense.

The only way to do a good radio sked is to warm up the batteries. "Hugh, could you put the batteries next to the stove while you're cooking?"

"Why don't you just ask me to run back to Resolute with a message for Elaine?" Hugh replied, somewhat heatedly.

Thinking it was time to take a strong line, I said, "Why don't you just bloody well grow up?" There was a long silence in the tents. Mitch screwed his face up at me, as if to say, "Now you've done it."

Jock was first to chirp up. "That's amazing, that's the first bad words on the trip. We ought to celebrate."

I was annoyed, not because of the batteries, but the fact that when we started off at Eureka I gave this long speech about pulling together, emphasising team work. We were bound to be fractious and argumentative at the end of the day when we were all tired. I was ashamed and furious with myself. Having done all the lecturing on the subject, I had been the first to break.

"Hugh," I shouted, "I'm sorry. I was well out of order."

"I've already forgotten all about it. Pass the batteries through, and what soup would you like?" This team was the dog's balls.

Jock finally got through to Elaine. "We aroused a polar bear."

"Jock, please repeat."

"We aroused, A for Alpha, R for Romeo, O, Oscar, A, Alpha, S, Sugar, E, Echo, D, Delta."

An elongated American drawl from the radio enquired, "Aroused?"

"Roger, roger."

There was a pause, then Elaine said, "Jock, how do you arouse a polar bear?"

The whole tent collapsed with laughter.

We all slept apprehensively, aware that tomorrow would be another crucial day. Mitch said he was starving. As he had had me humming the Birdie Song all day, I got him back by saying, "How would you like a steak and chips?" just before he went to sleep.

He licked his face and grimaced.

Brain has gone. Today is Ashley's birthday! It seemed a very long day as I had next to no sleep. Since I was the only one awake during the first two hours of the day I made up the hot drinks before calling Hugh. Arctic foxes visited us during the night, tracks are everywhere.

The longest walk and ski yet. I love this place. I feel alive here, yet constantly aware that the Arctic is in charge. Cold hands continued to be my biggest problem, each stop means they get cold and then take some time to warm up as I work on them. Aches and pains come and go – will my body last? My head says, "You will make it." Blister on left heel and sore right shoulder but these are things I can cope with. We travel through ever changing landscape; later in the day ferocious, jagged mountains leave us in awe of this place. There is no one here but us and an abundance of wild life.

It was obvious how tired we had all become when the first bad words were exchanged between Kim and Hugh. However, the measure and maturity of these guys came through when apologies were made straight away, and there was no sulking or continued ill feeling. The incident was simply the result of sheer fatigue.

I can cope with much more now and gladly take on additional duties; but I must get more sleep.

Jock's press releases are comical, at times providing much amusement, but I would prefer not to have the press skeds in our tent at almost 11.00. p.m.! Can't wait to hold my family again,

131

their photographs lift me when I am low.

DAY 10 – Tuesday 14th April

Hugh's cooking surpassed itself this morning. It was one of those great-to-be-alive days. The temperature had risen to -18°C. Clear blue skies, beautiful flat ice, and stunning mountains all around. We knew today was the day. Thumb Mountain looked so close.

Some time after we started, Mitch lost another filling – not too good for him, but at least it shut his whistling up. We gradually drew past the mountains, advancing closer and closer to Thumb Mountain. I was almost frightened to go any further. Recalling Wally Herbert's account of his experiences in this area made me very apprehensive.

Having got to within five hundred metres of the entrance, we could see a seal basking in the sun. The surface of the ice looked crystal blue, giving the impression of being open water. I stopped the team. It looked solid, but I didn't want a repeat performance of the Magnetic Pole trip when I fell through the ice. It was Hugh's turn in front, so I asked him to make a large detour. He thought it looked quite safe, but whenever danger presented itself I had flashbacks of Neill's wife: that scared rabbit looking right at me and trusting me. No chances! I was not about to use up all our luck this early. I was sure we would need some before the end of the trip.

We finally hit land, and made our way up the scree to the river. We could now see down the valley, but the blue skies had disappeared. A cloud layer had come down and the wind had started to blow. We couldn't see anything at all. The route was obvious, just follow the braided streams. Occasionally, we would hit beautiful clear blue river ice. The paulks had a mind of their own. It was easy going, and we were making excellent progress. Was this giving us a false sense of security? We marched on. Every now and then we caught glimpses of ice caps when the cloud partially lifted. The wind was now blowing straight down the valley into our faces. We had done a great day. I couldn't ask for more. We would need all our strength tomorrow.

As we put up camp for the night, the wind really started to pick up. The team was now working so well together, tents went up, were battened down, radio's set up, food, clothing and equipment in without a single word said, and all within five minutes of stopping. Everyone knew tomorrow would be a big day. Hugh asked if we should have a double meal. Mitch sat bolt upright at the thought. "Sorry, fellas," I said, "who knows what Christmas will bring? Just think of that McDonald's with double fries when we get back." We had all lost a lot of weight by now. This was no place to go on a diet.

Day 10 – Mitch's Journal

We all began to move up the Sverdrup Pass – where we all knew the ice would stop and work begin in earnest. Even as we approached the end of the ice pan marking the transition on to Ellesmere Island, we were given our first taste of the labour that was to follow. In the distance the sight of a seal basking in the weak rays of the sun could only mean one thing – open water. As we neared the land the seal slid from sight. Beneath the ice we could see the tell-tale shimmer of water between us and the pass. It was in such situations that our research reading paid off.

133

We prepared our harnesses to ensure both a secure fit and quick release from our sledges. If we fell through the ice they might be a life saving anchor; however, in the unlikely event that both man and sledge broke through the ice, the quick release was vital to facilitate a climb out. For the same reason we left the rear bindings on our skis undone (we had cross country skis fitted with Berwin bindings to accommodate the large Mukluk boots, and had a toe and rear nylon strap to secure them to the foot). We released our hands from the ski stick wrist straps to allow us to slide our hands down to a position immediately above the basket and use them as ice "daggers" should we need to pull ourselves from the water.

A soaking in Arctic waters could kill in minutes. At best we would have to make camp immediately and heat the individual with spare dry clothes, numerous sleeping bags combined with heat from our own bodies and the cooking stoves. Drying boots and clothes would consume vital fuel and jeopardise the chance of a successful expedition.

In the event, luck stayed with us and good preparation saw us through this particular hazard. Nobody broke through the ice but the time penalty in negotiating this section of terrain was considerable.

Day 10 – Hugh's Journal

Today, due to a combination of one bag and frost dropping from the roof of the tent, we had a cold start. Neill woke at 6.50 a.m. and by 7.30 a.m., having had the forethought to fill two flasks the previous night, we had one brew and the breakfast

134

completed. We are eating too much breakfast but we have a large supply of oats. Breakfast this morning included left-overs from other bags.

Crux point approaches. How we fare during the next few days will decide the outcome of the expedition. Today, Jock set us off at a good pace heading for Thumb Mountain. We marched for hours. As with all things in the Arctic, it took longer than was expected. Approaching the turn into Fordlet, we spotted what appeared to be open ice. Leaving the paulk, I walked forward to discover that it was in fact water that had melted and refrozen. Although it seemed safe, Kim told me to take a wide arc. As a precaution we loosened ski bindings, paulk traces and took our hands out of the ski pole loops. Fortunately, the ice was 10/10. Into the pass area before the entrance is a river plain some one kilometre wide with no visible main course to follow the numerous sandbanks. Incredible patterns are created by the sand and ice. Where we found frozen parts of the river the pace increased considerably. But these were intermittent. The weather is very changeable with cirrus as a precursor to high winds from the West accompanied by a thick cloud cover. By 7.00 p.m. the wind was gusting to twenty miles per hour with a chill of -42°C. Finding a sheltered bank, I levelled off and got the tents in snug. With the increased warmth, the radio sked was completed in our tent. Elaine cannot always understand Jock. Jock is not always aware the message has been passed and confuses Elaine with more information. Last night was not too bad although I am waking more during the night.

The average guy in the street would describe the Arctic as flat and white with the odd iceberg or crevice. How wrong. Today we moved into a river valley, very difficult to cross because of the stone and gravel surface, yet at one point we walked for a mile or so on translucent blue frozen water. Configurates at intervals with amazing mounds where water had burst up through the river surface, spilled out and frozen.

We had set camp in very high winds, close to a massive ice wall dominating the side of the mountain. When the sun caught the ice at a certain angle, it glowed with an amazing blue light, making it appear to be alive. Breathtaking beauty in the midst of a wilderness. Running a full day behind schedule now. It seems unlikely that we will be home before the 25th April, too long to be away from those I love. Tiredness and injuries are causing some friction – I am not immune and snapped today over conflicting walking speeds. This is for my children, my wife and her grandad – I must finish it!

CHAPTER SEVEN

THE VALLEY OF DINOSAURS

DAY 11 – Wednesday 15th April

Last night we were hit by a storm so fierce we had to tie the outer and inner tents together to prevent the loss of the flysheet. I am becoming increasingly paranoid, worrying about food, injuries, weather, ice, etc. I think I must have been influenced greatly by Wally Herbert's account and was concerned at what we might find as we progressed. So far we have had it easy.

However, the Gods were smiling on us this morning. I opened the tent door to gaze at an amazing sight of cliffs and glaciers tumbling down into the valley floor.

Mitch shot out. "Christ, it looks like 'The Valley of the Dinosaurs'!" We were looking up the valley at the eerie and foreboding Witch Mountain. I felt as if it were something out of *Lord of the Rings*. What an experience! What an adventure! Pooh Bear with all his friends. The others crawled out and stood stunned by the sight.

Jock seized on the occasion to carry out a ceremonial burial of a sleeping bag. He seemed to be getting plenty of sleep.

We piled down to the river valley. "Watch out for dragons!"

The icefields gave the impression of being thousands of feet above us. No way would we be able to climb over them with paulks! I wonder if Hattersley-Smith, who had told us we could walk over the icefield, had been under the impression we were giants.

The river bed opened up again into beautiful flat ice. After three hours, we came to a large rubble belt at the edge of a glacier. We were looking for a lake. In order to reach this objective, we had to climb a one five hundred foot contour line. From previous experience we knew what that meant. Getting stuck into it we heaved and pulled our paulks through this rubble belt, to the base of the glacier snout.

The valley had closed in on us, the cliffs and mountains swallowed us up. Heave over one rock, heave over another rock. No way could a dog team climb these.

This was the point where Wally Herbert, travelling in the opposite direction to us, wrote:

"When Sverdrup discovered it, the glacier had blocked the valley; now there was a narrow, boulder-strewn passage of rock and ice between the rock wall and the ice face. This passage we negotiated the next day, back-packing, as we had done in the canyon, every item of gear save for the sleeping bags and the tent. These we manhauled on the sledges, filming as we went, and in twelve hours of almost continual hard labour we advanced the camp half a mile and cleared the last obstacle that lay between us and the sea ice of Bay Fjord."

We could now see the problem Wally had had. He would have had to hand-haul over this. We finally came to a constriction of cliffs, about four feet wide, with a waterfall of ice coming through the rocks. Hugh and I walked along the canyon.

"How does it look?" Neill asked when we returned.

There was a good chance, I thought, that with all of us pushing and pulling we should be able to do it one paulk at a time. The canyon and waterfall was about one hundred yards long.

"Is this the canyon?"

"I don't know."

Once we had climbed to the top of this small canyon we saw the valley opening up with Witch Mountain looking over us, but I was certain it would never have taken Wally Herbert nine days to get through. I really didn't know. Certainly, walking back, I could recognise the canyon from Wally's photographs. So, maybe! I pulled over the last boulder. Well, at least we had two pieces of good luck. First, this glacier snout was not blocking our way like it did with Sverdrup, so we didn't have to climb up the icefield, and second, we should manage this canyon easily.

Mitch came over. He looked very serious. "I think the trip's over." We all looked at him in shock.

"The bottoms of the paulks have been pulled out as we hauled them over the rocks."

I raced over. We turned every paulk over. They were all made from Kevlar, carbon fibre and a resin base. Indeed you could see our belongings inside, but to me they didn't look that bad.

For the first time on the expedition I felt my leadership had to be played carefully. Mitch was the gentle giant who everyone, including myself, looked up to. He could whip me at everything, and usually when he was serious about what he said, he was right.

"What are your thoughts, Mitch?"

"Well, we have just covered twenty miles of land crossing, and we have sledges that are falling apart. We have another forty miles of land to go including the crossing of Bach. I don't think they will last."

"OK, that's a good point. I think we have a serious problem. However, there is no way we can get a helicopter or Twin Otter in here to rescue us, so we will have to walk back out to Irene Bay. That's roughly the same distance as Flagler Bay, so why don't we head for Flagler? If the paulks are ruined we can double up loads and if all is lost, call the 'plane up in Flagler."

I looked at Mitch, praying he would agree. You could have cut the silence with a knife.

"Good thinking, Batman."

Hugh chipped in with, "We can always carry the sledges over the boulders."

Jock suggested we put the heavy items at the back of the sledge instead of the front.

Neill said, "Don't just look at them, lets get going!"

I now knew the team wanted success just as much as I did. One by one, each sledge was pulled through the canyon by a line of men along its length. Each paulk slithered along the frozen ice until, an hour later, we broke out onto the lake.

"I don't think this is the canyon," I said. "This is just the teaser. The canyon is at the end of this lake."

What it had taken Wally Herbert and his dogs twelve hours to do, we had completed in one hour.

We harnessed up again, and started to walk across the most amazing scene. The lake was surrounded by ice caps, dominated by Witch Mountain, and was nestled into a bowl. The ice was crystal clear, enabling us to look right through, apparently to a depth of fifty feet. I shuffled across. It was as if you were walking on a tight rope from one skyscraper to another. It began to give me vertigo, and I couldn't look down, preferring to look at the horizon as we walked on. I knew this was the lake that Wally took nine days to reach from the top of the canyon. And that was downhill – we would be going uphill.

As we gradually drew past Witch Mountain, I was almost paranoid with anticipation of what to expect in the canyon that lay ahead. I had read Sverdrup's account:

> " . . . the river fell in a steep waterfall into a canyon. We made an attempt to get down here, and crossed a large drift of snow into a fissure with perpendicular walls on both sides. The fissure became deeper and deeper the farther we went, and at last we saw nothing but a small strip of daylight above our heads. Suddenly it became narrower than the breadth of a sledge, and all further progress west by that way was cut off. We were obliged to turn and laboriously work our way back up to camp . . . "

Wally Herbert also wrote:

> " . . . although the canyon promised to be one of the most difficult obstacles we had ever encountered, we had at least satisfied ourselves that there was, that year, no alternative route across the bare ground or the plateau."

We were gradually drawn into a water system, with the slope of the hills gradually rising into cliff faces which became steeper and steeper. The wind was howling around the corners; the sun gave the rock a beautiful reddish hue. It was like Cheddar Gorge on a miniature scale. Eventually, the cliffs drew together to a distance of less than ten feet. We came across one pair of polar bear prints down the middle of the canyon. This gave us cause for concern. If a bear decided to put in an appearance while we were struggling through here, there would be little room for manoeuvre.

Progress was painfully slow. Each hummock we approached presented yet another unique challenge to our flagging energies.

Having no alternative, we pushed and pulled the paulks to gain ground, yard by yard. Mitch was finding it hard going, he was still pulling one hundred and sixty pounds. At each hummock he would lean forward into his harness and strain until the veins of his neck were standing out with the effort required to manhandle the sledge over.

We came to a junction where the route divided into two equally impressive canyons. A strong wind was funnelling its way through.

"Which way?"

"I don't know!"

This was all we needed. Time was not on our side, and denied us the luxury of choosing the wrong route. Failing to make the right decision would mean losing yet another valuable day. We were in no position to afford even half the time Wally took to negotiate this pass.

"Well, which way?"

"Procrastination is the thief of all time!"

"All right then, Mitch, Jock, Neill, take the left canyon for thirty minutes. Hugh and I will take the right."

Making our way slowly forward, Hugh and I found it difficult, even without the sledges. Our route took an upward slope bounded by cliffs, which at a number of places closed to four feet in narrows. We gradually worked our way up. It certainly looked as if it was open the whole way. We had not lost the bear prints, they were still in the middle of the pass. We returned to confer with the others.

"What's your canyon look like?"

"Open all the way."

Our reconnaissance had not answered anything. Which way? Do we take the chance of going two days down the left and turning back or two days down the right and turning back? Climbing the cliffs was not a viable alternative. We stood and looked at each other.

I said, "Well, this might seem stupid, but let's take the polar bear route. Maybe he knows the easiest way!"

There was one consolation, at least we were not in Wally's position at this point, we hadn't got a bunch of yapping dogs and one thousand pounds to back pack. I had admired Wally Herbert for years. He and his team deserved medals just for negotiating this obstacle. In fact, the more we got into our trip, the more impressed I became with his, with all its trials and tribulations. It was arduous enough even though we were only pulling small paulks.

The decision made and agreed, we set off to follow our "bear guide". It became increasingly difficult to make ground. Pulling with all our weight, and with someone pushing from behind, we made slow progress. It felt as if we had already climbed five hundred feet.

Wally had even found time to film and take snap shots. We were just so tired, nobody could be bothered. Aching in every muscle, we struggled on for another four hours. I had but one prayer – "Please let this be the right route!"

The cliffs suddenly closed to a two foot gap. It looked a dead end. Vertical cliffs surrounded us one hundred and fifty feet high. Coming to a halt, I undid my harness, while the others pulled their sledges up to mine. I decided to carry out a reconnaissance. I walked up and up into the throne room of the Gods, and I could see blue sky ahead, with ice caps descending. The cliffs started to decrease in height. After an hour I eventually came onto what seemed another junction, but this looked like the top, with another canyon going into the valley. Was this the route or not? Hugh popped his head around the corner.

"Well it looks like the route, but I still can't be sure. Let's try to get here and camp."

"No way, Mitch and Jock have had it."

I was extremely concerned at Hugh's comment. In all my running, climbing and walking days with Mitch I had never known him to be bushed. I returned to find the tents up in the middle of the canyon. Along the way we had counted seven vertical lifts we would have to negotiate the next day.

Neill already had the food on.

"You OK, Mitch?"

"Would be, if we had some food."

They were all concerned that we might not be going in the right direction.

"It looks like the right way, but I really don't know."

As the canyon was less than five hundred feet nothing was shown on the map. We didn't even bother to put the Argos and radio on, knowing that with the high cliffs we would have no chance of reception. Looking up at the cliff face, I realised that if an avalanche came down, or a rock broke off, we would be mincemeat in the morning. There was not the least chance that a helicopter or aircraft would find us. Overhanging cliffs were too close to allow us even to fire a flare out. The situation was potentially very dangerous and it was imperative that we feed and rest up in order to be fit to extricate ourselves the next day.

In spite of our perilous position, it was certainly the most impressive camp site yet.

Mitch was so tired he even found it hard to eat his food. What was I doing to the fellas? They had each given one hundred and ten per cent. What else could we do? I just couldn't sleep. This place was so dangerous. If somebody broke a leg or an arm, what would we do? It would be serious stuff. Suppose a bear decided to re-trace its steps through the pass? It would be confronted with two tents taking up the whole of the gorge. Its only way down would be through us. I prayed and prayed for help.

"Pete, if you're looking down on me, please help me." Peter was my uncle who had died a few years previously. He would have loved this trip. He always reminded me of Steve McQueen. Cool as a cucumber, nothing was a problem. "Pete, help me get through this."

Day 11 – Mitch's Journal

As I awoke on day 11, I remember thinking that we had survived the most dangerous night so far. Erecting the tents last night was hazardous to say the least. A savage wind was channelled and accelerated down the pass, freezing everything in its path.

We had become very proficient at making camp – each man had naturally adopted his own role and got on with the job in hand. Last night however, the wind changed all that. Whilst Hugh dug the scrape in which to place the tents, the rest of us got on with assembling the flailing mass of nylon and aluminium. There was an urgent need to get out of the lethal gale as soon as possible, but at the same time we had to make a conscious effort to slow down our actions. To remove our cumbersome mittens in the wind would mean a night of pain trying to rewarm them, yet piecing the tent poles together was like threading a needle whilst wearing boxing gloves. A single mistake might mean the loss of a tent. We could survive the night with one tent, but not much longer than that. Evacuation from the pass was out of the question, since there was nowhere for an aircraft to land.

Morale was high as we headed our way along the pass in the footsteps of Sverdrup. Every now and then we would be treated to the luxury of river ice upon which to walk. We marched over a layer of clear blue ice, often as much as three feet thick and giving the impression that the river had been frozen in an instant during the autumn prior to our walk. As my sledge glided effortlessly behind me I began to wonder if the ice would taste minty if I licked it. Terrain in the Arctic is never the same for long however and we were soon hauling sledges over much more difficult country. In places it consisted of small round boulders such as seem to comprise the bottom of many mountain passes, interrupted by what I thought looked like giant sheets of sandpaper. Probably some form of volcanic debris, it was razor sharp. As we walked I became increasingly conscious of a familiar smell, evoking memories of the school workshop where we used to build canoes – I realised it was fibreglass resin. Whilst the rest of the group walked on I stopped to inspect the bottom of my sledge. My worst fears were confirmed – although the sledges had strengthened runners along their length, the structure of the fibreglass either side was damaged. Tracked down the length of my sledge were deep scores that had broken through the hard resin outer coating to expose the more vulnerable glass matting interior. The smell of the bonding resin was incredible. As I continued along the pass to catch up with the rest of the team I did a quick mental appreciation. The terrain over which we were walking was marked on the map as a type of Moraine field. My sledge was damaged but the effects would not be too severe if we could get back, and then remain on snow and ice. I recalled studying the map last night – there were four other such Moraine fields between us and the Kane Basin. The prospects did not seem too good, yet as I pondered our situation the going got worse with the snow and ice disappearing completely, leaving me with no option but to pull my battered sledge over the top of sharp stones and boulders. Ahead of me the lads had stopped where the pass had narrowed to a couple of metres. Kim and Hugh had left their sledges and gone forward to look at the terrain whilst Neill and Jock sheltered from the wind. Unhooking my sledge, I rolled it over to check the damage again. What I saw horrified me. The half mile travelled since the previous check had considerably worsened the damage. It was possible to see through a crack stretching for over twelve inches and the rest of the base looked pretty badly off too. I carried out a quick check on the other sledges. All were damaged, but to my relief, not as badly as my own. Being the sledge with the heaviest load it had understandably taken the roughest ride, but

Hugh's and Neill's would not last long at this rate.

The prospects looked even worse as I sat alone with my thoughts waiting for Kim and Hugh to return. None of us was carrying excess baggage which could be ditched to lighten the loads. Having decided against rucksacks we were left with no alternative way of carrying the kit. It was not possible to carry the sledges and if the map proved to be accurate we still had four more boulder fields to negotiate. Even if we decided that new sledges would have to be obtained by resupply, we would have to retrace our steps back through the Pass, and there was no way my sledge would survive that journey.

For the first time since the start of the expedition the seeds of doubt as to our success were beginning to form. My first thoughts were about the prospect of failing and returning empty-handed, and then turned to a little boy and his parents back home in England.

My wife Jackie had wanted to make the expedition work for charity as well as our own purely selfish goals of personal achievement. With this in mind, I had decided to raise money for a local boy born with Cerebral Palsy. Initially it had been a good cause, but as the days had gone by it increasingly became the driving force behind me. It was vital that this little lad should get the money people all over England and Germany were working to raise. For all that work and effort to come to nothing because of the failure of a piece of fibreglass was just not fair.

When Kim and Hugh returned I outlined the various options open to us. I was relieved and delighted when it took the lad all of two seconds to decide upon going on regardless. Not that this prevented me from constantly worrying over the next

148

two days that my sledge was at any moment about to spew its contents over the Sverdrup Pass.

Route finding now became even more laborious. Picking the easiest and shortest path between two horizons ceased and I was forced to haul my sledge around detour after detour, making the most of any available snow and ice in order to make the ride a little easier for my sledge.

My mind eventually returned to the task in hand and getting through the pass. As we moved further into the heart of Ellesmere Island the valley walls got higher and higher and the path at the bottom narrower. We worked like Trojans for the rest of the day, mindful that we were now behind schedule and were going to have to crack it up a bit. As each hour passed and at each break taken, I began to loiter as we set off again – there were rich pickings to be had from the ground as a carelessly eaten Monster Bag might reveal a piece of biscuit, or a raisin – all were gratefully accepted as I trawled the halt area for titbits before moving on to catch the boys for the next hour of punishment.

Good progress was made through the Sverdrup Pass and we are now midway across the island. So far we have all been able to pull our paulks but as we came close to the valley sides, which had now become canyon walls, they began to close in on us. By six o'clock that evening we found ourselves at the bottom of a gorge four feet wide and over two hundred feet high. In front of us lay a series of snow drifts we would have to climb, each one involving a lift of at least twenty feet. To make matters worse we knew we would have to make camp in this gorge as we were too tired at the end of a long day to make that sort of climb; furthermore we had passed several sets of large polar bear prints entering the gorge. When erected side by side our two tents left no room for anything to pass our encampment. Should any bear be out at night travelling our route it would walk right into the tents! The rifle was double checked and left readily available. That evening we did not even attempt to make our scheduled contact with base over the radio. Communication would be almost impossible due to the screening effects of the gorge and erecting the dipoles for the HF radio was a laborious task that exposed fingers to the wind. It didn't take much to convince ourselves that the task was futile and that our base crew would predict the problem and not become too worried.

Day 11 – Neill's Journal

Today we started a very difficult walk along ice with no snow cover, easy for pulling paulks but a bitch for keeping your balance. Moved steadily upstream until we had to cross rocks and boulders which did significant damage to our paulks and caused Mitch some concern. The route took us to the edge of the ice field that almost cut off our only entrance to the gorge. The gap was reduced to about twenty feet. Moving on, we manhauled our paulks up waterfalls and snow banks, perceiving this to be the section of the "Sverdrup Pass" described by Wally Herbert, which opens on to the high level Black Water lake.

We feel we have reached a crossroad in the expedition when we realise that we have yet to climb the Sverdrup Pass Gorge. There was some debate over directions – tiredness producing friction again which is rapidly diffused with humour. We enter a gorge not more than fifty feet across and about sixty feet high, and carry out some reconnaissance before deciding to set camp as we are too tired to carry on. This was my favourite camp so far with no radio contact or Argos.

So – tomorrow is "Crunch Day". I'll go on because I have set my mind to the idea that my children and Lindsey are on the other side. I really feel part of this enterprise. Sheer excitement is only tinged by missing my family. I hurt everywhere but this body will get me through – I hope! Kim is very nervous, almost seeming insecure at present. He has this great responsibility on his shoulders but we are a team and will share the load. Poor Mitch is as homesick as me.

I am now relied on more and more, it's a good feeling. I will never forget Hugh's encouragement. In fact they are all inspirational in their own way. Mitch, the gentle giant, is always calm and offering considered opinions or advice. Kim has extremely broad shoulders. I hope he is aware of how much I thank him for this chance. Jock, the source of much amusement, I am happy to help him with anything.

CHAPTER EIGHT

THE BLUE BRICK ROAD TO THE POLE

DAY 12 – Thursday 16th April

I was up at the crack of dawn. Neill had breakfast on. We gulped down our food, after which Hugh and I retraced our steps to make an assessment of what was involved in negotiating the vertical lifts. On our return, the team was eager to move on. We decided the best method of making progress would be to have two of the team at the top pulling, and three at the bottom pushing up. Being psychologically sold on the idea that getting the heaviest sledge over first would make lighter ones appear to fly over, we decided Mitch's sledge would be first in line.

On the way down through the canyon, Hugh showed me his hands. Three fingers appeared to have suffered bad frostnip. Although he felt he would be OK, I was very concerned. I asked him to give me a twice daily check. He didn't want anyone else to know, so as not to worry them.

We lined the five sledges up at the bottom of the first vertical lift, about six feet, through a narrow gap. Mitch and Hugh hauled while the rest of us pushed.

"Jesus!"

"Bloody hell!"

"You bastard!"

It was at this stage, we discovered Mitch's sledge weighed about two hundred pounds! A total surprise to everyone except him. Hugh's and mine each weighed roughly the same, about one hundred and twenty pounds. Jock's and Neill's weighed in at probably eighty pounds. We would have to redistribute this weight on reaching the top.

It was hard work. We heaved, pushed, tugged and pulled. We used our knees, arms, legs and shoulders. It was fantastic. After each lift:

"Yeah, yeah – get angry with it."

There was a brilliant team spirit. Seven to go, six to go, five to go, and so on . . .

Neill was in his element. This situation demonstrated more than anything so far, the significant change in this young man. He had established himself as an essential and important member of the team. Everyone recognised how he had grown in stature.

After what seemed to be an eternity of grinding sweat and toil, we heaved over the final lift. At last, we had reached the high point where Hugh and I had stood the previous day. We quickly donned harness and raced down the lesser canyon, which had widened with cliffs now reduced down to approximately twenty feet. Hugh kicked up to the top of a long snow slope.

"I can see the valley in front of me!"

We quickly roped our sledges up this final slope.

"Don't break a leg now!"

With the last sledge up, we belted for some rocks. From the top we could see Witch Mountain behind us, and Flagler Bay in the distance. We thumped each other on the back. We had beaten the canyon in one day. We were still on schedule. "Thanks Pete!"

It would be wrong to make any comparison between the two expeditions, since they differed in many ways, but we were quite chuffed to have taken roughly one day to complete a distance which had taken Wally Herbert, with his dog team, a total of nine days. Having now made the journey ourselves, we were all surprised it hadn't taken them much longer. Man-hauling every item up and down a giant obstacle course was not my idea of fun. We quickly made our way up to the watershed of Ellesmere, a plateau from where we could see the mountains in every direction. Witch Mountain was getting further away. It was a completely new environment this side of the valley, warm and friendly compared to the harsh, cold, and stunningly sharp scenery of the West coast. We were now noticing musk oxen droppings and evidence of grass, sure signs of other vegetation under the snow.

Gradually making our way downhill, we pushed on until what looked like an orange tent came into view. As we drew closer, we could see it was a parkall hut that belonged to the Polar Shelf. Getting to within one hundred yards, we hollered and yelled. The last thing I wanted was to creep up on two scientists who might mistake our knocking on the door as a visiting polar bear. We drew closer. The lads walked in. I stayed outside, feeling this contact to be an intrusion of our freedom. Meanwhile, I could hear the fellas rattling around. It wasn't long before my curiosity got the better of me. Walking through the door, I could see the site had been left by scientists the previous year. A log book was in place, plus a shotgun. Neill penned a message to our absent friends. There was something strange about coming into contact with semi-civilisation in the middle of such a desolate and lonely place. Everyone was quiet for some time.

We were now making good progress downhill. We had a large alluvial plain in front of us, and were meandering from one side of the valley to the other in order to pick our way on to the snow and ice and safeguard the bases of our sledges. The wind had picked up, and was thundering down from the icefields behind us. We were all exhausted. We stopped on the hour for a hot drink.

"How are you feeling?"

"No problem."

"One hundred per cent."

"Go all day."

"Keep going."

It was obvious that we were all weak from hunger; tired and aching from pulling and wrenching, and just plain worn out and run down. But not beaten! What a team! How could anyone ask for more? Whenever I decided it was to be the last hour, everyone seemed to perk up, cheered by the fact we would soon be in our maggots. We had worked ourselves into a routine of walking, eating and sleeping and that was it. Our day revolved around these three activities. The last hour flew by. Our spirits were high because we were all aware it was downhill from here. We knew each other so well that even with the wind biting into us, we had camp up and the stoves going within ten minutes of stopping. Jock was again up until the wee hours trying to do his radio sked. He is so professional and determined once he sets his mind to do something. As for the rest of us, it was head down and dream of baked beans on toast.

With five men on each paulk, the morning was spent hauling ourselves step by step out of the gorge. By lunch time we could once again see the tops of Ellesmere Island. In the space of some three hours we had travelled about half a mile. With the sun providing some warmth to cheer us up we set off Eastwards. The going continued to be difficult and we were constantly having to pick our way through a boulder strewn river bed. At this stage all the sledges had been holed to varying degrees due to the punishing stony surface. Mine developed a split which travelled the full length of the fibreglass hull. This caused me some concern, but with our options being strictly limited it was decided to carry on in the hope that the sledge would survive the distance. During the afternoon as we topped the island, we came across an isolated weather reporting station. Consisting of a single prefabricated hut set in the middle of this Arctic wasteland, it was the lonely refuge of two weather researchers during the summer months. We penned a hasty note of greeting to the next incumbents and left. The effects of stumbling across signs of humanity again after two weeks isolation from civilisation remained with and haunted me for the rest of the day. The discipline I had imposed on myself to maintain an efficient routine of walking, eating, sleeping, had been thrown into confusion by the sight of a couple of steel beds and armchairs in a makeshift house. Apparently I was not along in being thus affected. That night Kim wrote something similar in his log. It was now an established routine for Hugh, Neill and Jock to prepare the evening meal and drinks in one tent, whilst in the other tent Kim and I carried out the required scientific readings, plotting our position and the distance travelled that day. The moment when the evening meal was prepared was always one to savour, but the highlight of the evening came when we got a satellite fix on the Global Positioning System (GPS) and could calculate the distance we had yet to walk in order to reach the Pole.

Day 12 – Elaine May's Journal

No radio Contact. Team in the Sverdrup Pass.

All the pilots and engineers in the complex have taken an interest in the expedition. Often a couple of them will join Shirley and me in the kitchen when we make our broadcast. Once in a while, they will take over the transmission and try to convey some important information when reception is bad. It never fails to amaze me how they are able to make sense out of what sounded to me like 10/10 squab. I guess it comes from years of experience. Tonight, we failed to get any reception. However, we are not too worried because we know the team are in the middle of a deep gorge.

Day 13 – Friday 17th April

We had broken camp, and were ready for the off. As normal we huddled around to discuss the day's objective.

"Another crux day. We need to try and get to Flagler Bay by tonight to keep us up with our new schedule."

Jock was still optimistic about going twenty miles per day. The world record for a day's run was held by Wally Herbert's dog team. He did twenty-three miles, so we had some hope!

There was one notable behavioural change. Whereas on the first day each individual walked fifty yards away to take a whizz, now while I was doing the quick morning brief, everyone stood in the circle and took a whizz – usually aiming for my boots! Maybe that's what they thought of the day ahead, but it showed that our inhibitions had gone. We had become much closer as a team in so many ways. Now we were able to talk to each other openly about our fears of not making it: our families, our careers, etc.

It was downhill again. However, we had to negotiate a huge river system, wandering through massive mountains. We were following the bed of a young river, with meandering curves, and steep gradients which would be white water during the summer months. Through beds of huge stones we picked our way cautiously to avoid any further damage to the sledges. We had re-distributed some of the weight from Mitch's sledge, but he was still pulling the heaviest load by far. I kidded that Hugh and Mitch should have the heaviest loads as the rest of us had stumped up the taxes to pay for their service training which had kept them fit. We were considering jettisoning some of our extra kit such as old batteries and useless clothing, but we decided to carry them the whole way so as not to spoil these beautiful surroundings with our litter.

Out of the wind, it was -20°C and beautifully warm, just like a Scottish winter. As we dropped down to sea level the cliffs rose in stature and we seemed to come across more and more wildlife. Arctic foxes, hares and musk oxen were wandering around. It was a long, long day. We had been pushing hard once again, and had now entered into a zone of huge rocks. I was desperate to get to Flagler. I could see the cliffs of the bay in the distance, but we were moving so slowly, having to pick our way, that I thought we had no chance.

On turning a corner, I realised our dreams had been answered. A beautiful blue road of hard river ice was descending as far as I could see. We were skating around like little kids. I turned to see Mitch flying past me, sitting on top of his sledge, nonchalantly doing the Queen's wave as he went! No stones, no grit, just ice. Lovely, lovely blue ice. Progressing at a good four miles an hour, with little effort being required to pull our sledges, Flagler Bay gradually came into view. We kept going at a tremendous pace until we came to the bar where sea ice met river ice. We headed over to the shoreline. This must count as one of the most beautiful camp sites in the world, surrounded by steep cliffs in all directions. Everyone was upbeat that night. Only seventy-eight miles to go. It hardly seemed possible.

Jock was on the radio to Elaine.

"Here we go, Elaine . . . "

"Where's he going, Mitch?"

"Order the 'plane up for four days' time. Tuesday night."

"No, no, no! Don't do that!"

"If we do four days at twenty miles per day, we can do it."

"And what if we don't? Let's order up the 'plane when we know for sure."

It seemed unbelievable that we were actually now starting to talk about a pick-up.

Mitch rifled in his maggot. "Kim, write this down: Waypoint Oscar to Juliet, Waypoint Whisky to Yankee, Waypoint Zulu to

Alpha?" This was pilot jargon for distances worked out on the GPS for a known point to another known point. "Listen up. We have seventy-eight miles to go."

Last summer Mitch and I had run the eighty mile World Trail Championship in under twenty hours. "Hey, Mitch," I said, "if we ditch everything we could make a run for it and get a McDonald's at the Pole." What a thought! Poor Mitch, the very mention of food made him drool.

We were now discussing in earnest the re-arranging of our route. We were supposed to cross the Bach Peninsula and get into the Kane Basin well North of the ice bridge, which was quickly eroding away. Elaine had told us she had flown to Thule with her father and the rest of the American group, and could confirm the bridge to be moving North. We were worried that a long haul over a nine hundred feet pass would drain us all, and damage the sledges beyond repair. It was decided to keep to the Southern route and follow the coast of the Bach Peninsula to Cape Camperdown and then head North.

"OK, Jock, get on to Elaine," I said. "Tell her we have changed the route, and tell her not to forget some beers when she comes in. Lads, I owe you all a pint. We took three and a half days to cross Ellesmere. If we had not been delayed by the reconnaissance detour down the other canyon, it would have been three days."

"I'll drink to that," said Hugh as he shoved a piping hot cup of soup into my hand.

DAY 13 – Hugh's Journal

Night is not just for sleeping – it is for cold feet! Did not sleep well last night but this expedition has taught me to put away the

Ascent to the Gorge.

Camped in the Gorge.

Walking in the Gorge

Coming out at the top.

Sunset on the clear blue ice -
"the blue brick road to the Pole".

Packing always takes twice as long as unpacking.

Beautiful flat ice to Flagler Bay.

weariness I feel and persevere – although this morning getting up was difficult. Jock's boots are causing him some trouble, he is presently trying to melt the ice inside them in order to free the inners. In his haste to sort his boots problem Jock burnt them. Fortunately it is not too bad. The inners are now out and hopefully this will give him several days' respite. All the team want to reach Flagler Bay by tonight. In a straight line it is a distance of fourteen miles but we must conform to the course of the river to avoid low snow coverage on the surrounding hills. This could extend the march to twenty miles, a distance we have yet to achieve! Each morning sees Jock looking increasingly exhausted. He is getting some sleep, but it is intermittent.

I led the first pull. It consisted of some river ice but was mostly snow-covered pebbled moraine. Being very conscious of the state of the paulks, the route I take is quite torturous. Nevertheless we are getting there. Mitch took the next lead and within five miles had found the Blue River Road. River ice all the way down to the sea. Having experienced some tough hauls it was a great relief to have the paulks moving over this surface almost of their own accord. A strong wind has been blowing all day, gusting to twenty miles per hour, with an ambient temperature of -20°C. At this strength the wind seems capable of blowing through the wind suit – to such an extent that my arms become next to useless because I delay too long in putting on my fleece.

There is now some discussion about the route. Whether to go over the Bach, or to go along the sea ice to Cape Albert, and then on to the Pole; a distance of seventy-eight miles. The big question is – can we make twenty miles a day and complete in four days? As a rough calculation:

8 hours @ 2.5 m.p.h.= 20 m.p.d.

Departure 10.00 a.m. – Arrival 7.00 p.m. = 9 hours march

9 hours @ 2.5 m.p.h. = 22.5 m.p.d.

$$\frac{78 \text{ miles}}{22.5 \text{ m.p.d.}} = 3.5 \text{ marching days (3 days 4 hours)}$$

We could be picked up on Tuesday about mid-day.

It has been decided to use the Southern route. If we finish on Tuesday it will have taken a total of seventeen days. On the 24th April, we will run out of food! Unfortunately we will not be able to return to Britain until Sunday due to the Friday flight schedules.

DAY 14 – Saturday 18th April

I was staring at the ceiling of the tent, waiting for the fifteen minute countdown while our flasks were being readied, signalling the time for me to get out of my maggot. Suddenly, my bowel was having contractions. I just couldn't hang on for the fifteen minute call from next door to break camp. Dressing in some haste, I crawled out. It was -20°C, no wind, and we were surrounded by cliffs. Just wonderful. Must have been the most scenic dump I've ever had. Before I got back, my sledge had been packed.

162

Again Jock said, "Twenty miles today." It would be nice to do it just once on the trip.

We were off at a hell of a pace, on ice as flat as a billiard table, when I noticed Neill hobbling. "Stop!" We were going so fast, we all shunted into each other. It transpired that Neill's cartilage had gone. Considering the implication of Neill's injury, I recalled an incident on my Duke of Edinburgh's Bronze award. We were given a time and place at which we were to report to Mr. James. Realising we had no hope of making time as a group, I shot off without the team. I reported in – "Where's the rest, boyo?"

"Don't know, sir."

"All for one and one for all. You succeed or fail together."

Protestations of getting to the checkpoint on time fell on deaf ears. The ignominy of getting the slipper in front of all of those mountain sheep never left me. Neither has the lesson the occasion taught me.

Every member of this team was going to know the sweet taste of success, or, share equally the disappointment if it failed. Hugh strapped Neill's knee and dosed him with pain killers. I now wished we had brought more. In order to cope with my Achilles problem, I had increased my dose, taking two every two hours. Supplies were running low. Mitch got down to unloading Neill's sledge, and re-packing it into the others.

"Neill, you lead, and don't go at a stupid pace. We go at your pace and your pace only. If you can't manage it, we can put you in the sledge and pull you, failing that, we'll take it in turns to piggy-back you to the Pole."

Once again I thought, what was I doing to this team? I felt like a football coach, when one fellow breaks down, get another in front. Play all your options. We were all suffering from fatigue, each of us now carrying an injury in one form or another. No one complained except me. I felt I had to moan for all of us. Extra weight from Neill's sledge was killing me, until Mitch re-positioned the heavy weight into the back of the sledge. Thank God one of us was thinking straight. You would never think such a simple solution could make that much difference. How that animal Mitch had pulled all that weight this far, I will never know. We all weighed considerably less than when we set out, and were so exhausted that any loss of weight in the paulks made little difference. In spite of his injury, Neill still allowed us to make excellent progress.

Mitch was getting the Trimble nice and warm. Sticking to our original schedule, we would have arrived at the Pole tomorrow. Hugh was now getting worried about food, telling me, "We are now breaking into emergency food."

The radio sked was poor that night. I hoped our radio batteries were OK. Elaine was so good. She's such a bright girl. We were lying in our bags with our noses sticking in the air, listening to Jock struggling with poor RT reception at Base.

"Jock, I can hardly hear you. I'm going to assume you can hear me, and will give you the Argos position and weather forecast."

"Good girl."

She had been nicknamed Resolute Rose. Her voice sounded so good after a day's hard slog. It had a warmth that we were missing, and it was a glimpse of civilisation which we were beginning to pine for. Jock asked me if we should get the 'plane in for Wednesday night. "We have just over sixty miles to go. That's fifteen miles a day. We've been doing that most days."

"No, don't tempt fate."

I looked out of the tent. Snow was falling. "Jock, look outside, Father Christmas just went by."

Day 14 – Hugh's Journal

TEMP: -2°C

WEATHER: Blue skies with sun – but snow halfway down the bay in the form of ice crystal cloud.

Mother's birthday. I have asked Elaine to 'phone and wish her Happy Birthday. The day started well and within two and a half hours we had covered some eight miles when disaster stuck. Neill, who had had a bad fall the previous day, told us his knee was painful. He believed it to be due to a previous cartilage problem. I put a tubi-grip on the knee and suggested that I could immobilise it, but Neill was keen to manage with the tubi-grip and go on. We continued to march at a reasonable rate along the bay and it was obvious that Neill's knee was hurting him. I have damage to the little toe on both my feet by what I thought were blisters, but they seem to be bruised and are very painful. Kim's ankle is bothering him more and more. He is taking codeine every four hours, a treatment which is becoming less and less effective, but he must maintain the schedule, at least in the near future. We all looked to the next camp with eager anticipation. Tents up, we had a meal which included the last of our soup – the Bovril has come in handy! No peas for the evening meal, so I bulked it up with Breakfast. Never again will I cut corners with rations. At the end of each day we now make camp almost "out of fuel" and due to having to stretch available supplies do not receive a "full tank" to take us through the following day.

Tonight we are not feeling so good, we seem to have had a day of injury and obstacles. There are still four days' march ahead of us. The distance given to us last night was calculated on a straight line. This means a Thursday pick-up! Jock met with no success in getting his press release across – we will try again tomorrow.

Day 14 – Neill's Journal

Although I woke with the usual aches and pains, everyone was in a good mood and the routine of breaking camp went well. We started off well, or so it seemed, but we were hit with some snags as the day progressed. Kim's ankle is troublesome and still requires a daily dose of pain killers. Hugh is very tired and anxious to get the job finished; as are we all. Mitch is obviously suffering from lack of food but he never complains. As we walked I had very negative thoughts, mainly surrounding work, but more specifically Lindsey's grandad who is gravely ill in hospital. Then my knee began to hurt and within two hours was too painful to bend. I couldn't believe it – an old football injury had come back to haunt me! We stopped on the hour and I told the team of my problem. No panic! Hugh put an elastic bandage on my knee and said if it got any worse they would strap my leg so that it would not bend. They then split my load between them and I switched my harness to my shoulders and struggled on. There are still some sixty miles to go, how could fate let me go this far, find flat ice and then let this happen? Come what may, I will finish.

Kim is a bit upset about pick-up arrangements, feeling that Borek are ripping Jim May off by insisting on two 'planes.

Please don't let anyone say we will do twenty miles today! Every time it works against us.

DAY 15 – Sunday 19th April

We left at 10.30 a.m. I wished we could get one really early morning, but how could I complain? Neill insisted on having all of his kit back. He looked like a bean pole. On 6000 calories a day, I'd lost about twenty pounds so far. Mitch's eyes looked hollow. Neill and Jock were now beginning to be affected by lack of food. I was also a little worried about the ice bridge. I hoped we could make Cape Camperdown before the ice broke away. If we had to do a large detour North, it would really kill us.

It had warmed up considerably. I was sure it was -15°C or warmer. For the first time, we walked without head protection and without gloves. My nails had grown too long since we started, and I had a couple of cold blisters on my fingers, but nothing to shout about. My stomach felt queasy that day. Hugh thought it was the effect of all the pain killers on an empty stomach. I hoped we would make it soon, as we were almost out of tablets, and no way could I walk without them. My ankle was swollen to double its normal size. Hugh was doing well, keeping it going.

We gradually drew closer to some nanatucks at the end of the

Knud Peninsula, looking like islands in the middle of the sea. Polar bear prints were all around. The reason soon became apparent – open water. It stretched right across our path, with the exception of a thin bridge across the middle. Hugh was keen on crossing. Again I remembered the Magnetic Pole expedition when I went through the ice. Having made good progress that day, however, it was very tempting. I felt it my responsibility to take the lead. The very thought of crossing the surrounding ice made me feel sick. I just hate thin ice. Anything but thin ice!

We were just putting on our skis when a couple of seals popped up and looked around. In terms of wildlife, we had now seen most things. This vast barren land was a naturalist's dream. We made a huge detour around the ice which took two hours out of the day. In terms of terrain, we had also seen everything. Everything except really bad polar pack ice – but there was still time for that! I switched the lead between Mitch and Hugh, who both made good time. We were now drawing into Buchanan Bay and for the first time, the coastline stretched down to our right. In the far distance we could see the high snow-capped mountains of Greenland. We were very close to the Kane Basin. Would nature be kind to us?

That night, Elaine sounded worried about open water. We gave her our orders for food on the pick-up. Jock still wanted to order the 'plane up for Wednesday. Mitch worked out we still had sixty-one point seven miles to go. Due to the two hour detour, it had been one of our longest days out on the ice.

"How far, how far?"

I didn't want to hurt them. "Still sixty miles, but just."

I was trying to sew up a hole in my glove. "Mitch, how do you do this?" He got so frustrated at seeing a cack-handed goon trying to sew,

168

he did it for me. "While you're at it, you couldn't sew up my boxer shorts?"

"Push off."

Day 15 – Hugh's Journal

Breakfast is now finished – right on schedule. We now have oats for breakfast, supplemented by monster bags. All food is running low, but as long as we can complete on Thursday we will still have some to spare. Today has been annoying due to Neill's injury. Jock's pace was too slow even for Neill! As time went by the pace was increased to a point where we seemed to be within grasping distance of the elusive twenty mile target. Then I noticed open water ahead, two polynyas between the Bach and a large island. Going forward without my paulk I saw two seals playing in the right hand polynyna, and, observing the ice to be very grey, decided to retreat. It was decided to bypass the area to the right. Kim took the lead and we spent the next two hours working our way round numerous patches of grey ice, slush and open water. As we moved into multi-year I took the lead, at first moving gingerly, much as a cat crosses a pond on an unsafe plant, making my way on skis. It was taking too long. I removed the skis and walked forward – aware of the problems, but at least not fearing fear. We set a good pace from here and by 7.30 p.m. reached a point twelve miles from Cape Camperdown. Camp was set and food eaten. A discovery was made that marred the entire expedition. The thermometer I had borrowed from Robnor had broken. I had looked after it all this time and now it was gone. – Sorry!

Hugh has bound my knee and it is now fully supported. I have asked for, and got my load back. The first four hours went well enough, then the two sides of the bay closed in on a rocky headland, the ice became broken into patches of open water (Polynyas). Seals surfaced to gaze at the mad five on skis, gingerly picking their way round the thin ice. There cannot be too many guys who have gelled in the way we have. No one will ever understand what I am going through each day. Even if I stopped today I have proved something to myself. Both physically and mentally I have produced effort which I may never match again. I have got some wonderful friends here. No more crunchy nut cereal, it's oats and monster bag remains now. Tomorrow the sea ice.

DAY 16 – Monday 20th April

The tension was now rising. Everyone was pensive. Today our schedule was to get to Cape Camperdown. We had to succeed. It would be a shame to get this far, and have to get a re-supply because we were short of a couple of days' food. I won't leave this ice until I get to the Pole. Everyone was being abnormally polite. The suspense was killing us all. Would there be open water? We could see dark clouds to the South across the bay, a sure sign of open water. Trying to make progress on an empty stomach was hard work. We all eyed each other's monster bag to make sure no one had a bigger one.

"You've got more chocolate than me."

"Rubbish."

I consumed the contents of my monster bag in less than an hour. I even tried eating my Dextrose that day. I hated them, but sometimes necessity demanded it. Mitch came up with a new game – who could suck a Rolo the longest. I did twenty seconds, then swallowed it whole.

Mitch was now limping. He hadn't complained once. I was developing a heartfelt admiration for each member of the team, and felt so privileged just to be with them. They each had magnificent qualities. If I had put down all the ideal requirements of a team, they would have met them all.

With each hour that passed, we gradually drew closer and closer to the Cape. Each member of the team was starting to talk of home and family. Jock, probably the hardest egg of us all, sat on his sledge and said, "When I get home, I promise to read a bedtime story to Gregory and Laurie every night, especially the one about the teddy bears." The Arctic had taught us all a little something. We had the time to think, time to reminisce, time to realise what we had, what good lives we lead, how we took things for granted, especially our loved ones. Even though we had become quite good at ribbing each other, nobody said a word when Jock made the comment about his children. He said it from his heart. We were all now desperately homesick.

We passed Cape Camperdown. I could now see Victoria Head, and the mountains to the North of the Kane Basin. The Arctic would have its last say. We hit it with a thud. Pack ice! Ice rubble as far as the eye could see. We didn't have water, which was a God-send, but this ice formation would slow us up to half speed. We were looking at boulders ranging from the size of cars to the size of houses. I hadn't expected it to be this rough. I had only come across ice this bad at the top of Cape Columbia on my solo Geographical Pole trip.

Like ostriches with our heads in the sand, even though all evidence indicated we would be in for a terribly rough go, we all camped with the belief it would get better the next day. Less than forty miles to go according to the Trimble, Jock started to talk about getting home again.

"Jock, provisionally Wednesday, provisionally only. We will not leave this ice until we reach the Pole."

It was time for the next sked to Resolute Rose. "Elaine, don't forget the beef sandwiches with mustard."

Elaine came over the air loud and clear. "We can only get a ski 'plane to you Thursday."

Jock hit the roof. Hugh and Neill managed to calm him down. This delay would be better for us in terms of mileage, but it was cutting it close for food. What would happen if we got a storm?

I went to bed praying things would get easier. "I know I asked for solid ice, but please God, don't overdo it."

Day 16 – Elaine May's Journal

The Start of the Ice Sea.

Now that I have sorted out the time differences with the British reporters (having discovered that tired pilots don't really care for 'phone calls from overseas at two or three in the morning), I am becoming quite good at press interviews. I have come up with some standard bits of information the press are all interested in, such as:

172

"Their trip can be divided into three parts, with differing types of terrain. The first was the channel between Ellesmere and Axel Heiburg Island, which should be very smooth ice. As they began to cross Ellesmere Island through Sverdrup Pass, they encountered some rough going, with deep gorges and exposed rock to pass over. They are now entering on to rough sea ice, where they must deal with pressure ridges of up to thirty feet in height."

CHAPTER NINE

SO CLOSE BUT SO FAR

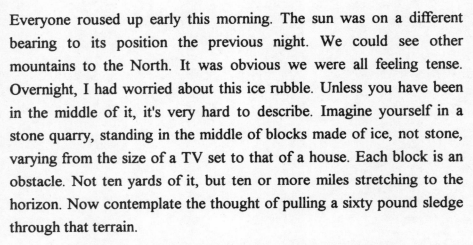

DAY 17 – Tuesday 21st April

Everyone roused up early this morning. The sun was on a different bearing to its position the previous night. We could see other mountains to the North. It was obvious we were all feeling tense. Overnight, I had worried about this ice rubble. Unless you have been in the middle of it, it's very hard to describe. Imagine yourself in a stone quarry, standing in the middle of blocks made of ice, not stone, varying from the size of a TV set to that of a house. Each block is an obstacle. Not ten yards of it, but ten or more miles stretching to the horizon. Now contemplate the thought of pulling a sixty pound sledge through that terrain.

We had forty miles to go. We had stretched the food to the limit, only three days remained – I even noticed Mitch trying to eat his emergency candle. The situation was critical. Should I expect my team to undergo something this rigorous? Where should I draw the line?

We broke camp quickly, under beautiful blue skies. "Pack your sledges tight," I said. "Keep it as small as possible. Tie the skis on top. Put a length of rope on my sledge and the ice axe in Hugh's, just in case somebody goes through. Keep Cape Albert behind us and head diagonally up the basin in line with Victoria Head. For the first day we won't need a check with the sun compass. Instead of stopping on the hour, carry on for another fifteen minutes. This will make the day longer, but we won't have to stop to make another set of flasks after these are used up."

Jock started off, straight into the rubble. Up, down, sideways, this way, that way.

"It looks easier over there, head for that block of ice."

"Oh yeah, smart ass, what block?"

"That one on the horizon."

We all stopped, looked around, and five men pointed in five different directions. I took the next lead. It was so slow it was pitiful, pulling up our sledges over each block. On my previous trip I had perfected the barrel roll with my paulk. After a few modifications to the packing of my sledge, I found I could repeat it. I was chuffed. "Look at this, lads." With a sharp pull on the right block, my sledge would turn in mid-air and land on its base. Brilliant. Even at this time of hardship and low spirits, we were still kids at heart.

With only three days of food left, we were humping no weight except our kit. No more than sixty pounds each. Jock took the next lead. The time was ticking by. Forty miles! We could never do it at this pace. I sat down on a slab of ice while Jock negotiated yet another pressure ridge. I put my head in my hands. I was overwhelmed with frustration. I could feel our success slowly being robbed from us. I had brought them this far, but for what? Surely not to fail?

We had only been travelling for a couple of hours, everyone was stunned at the complexity of the rubble. During the past three days each one of the team had come to me privately and voiced concern and worry. Did I really think we would do it? Even Hugh, who was normally up-beat, now had his doubts. As I looked around it was like the walking wounded, everyone silent, wondering which way next. I sat down. My face was burning from the wind, my eyes were sore, my nose was raw from loss of skin frozen to my glasses when I removed them. My backside was sore from walking. I had cold sores on the cheeks of my face, my Achilles tendon was still playing up. Every bone in my body ached. I had been one hundred per cent confident we would get to the Pole. Now, I was doubting we could get there even with a resupply. Bob Swan, on his ice walk expedition, averaged three and a half miles for the first ten days of his trip. That was with a fresh team on the ice. From my experience, this difficult terrain equalled anything I saw at Cape Columbia. If we averaged three and a half miles per day, we would never make the Pole without support. In fact, we would need another ten days and I wasn't sure if I or the others could do that. My chest started to get tight, my glasses began to blur and my eyes started to well up. Mitch must have subconsciously known how I was feeling, silently he came up behind me and, without saying a word, put an arm around my shoulder, squeezed it and walked on. Neill came over and said the lads were all behind me. My moment of despair and homesickness was gone. I was now fired up again. It was time to respond to this heartening support from the lads. "Right! When the going gets tough, the tough get going. Get angry with it, Jock."

We were stopping and starting, always catching up with the lead man. We were not going about this in the right way.

"Neill, take the lead for the rest of the day. I don't want to catch you. Don't go so far that you're in danger, but get a gap between us. We need something to chase."

It did the trick. He shot off and we never caught him.

My stomach rumbled all day long. Maybe it was the thought of all that food coming in on the pick-up flight. We did a gruelling nine and a half hours, one of our longest days, and yet completed the shortest distance, just over eight miles. We had done more than that on the land crossing.

That night we lay in our sleeping bags, with less than the distance of a marathon to go. From my home, I have a regular running route. In an attempt to visualise the distance we had yet to travel, I traced and re-traced every step of every mile. So close. So desperately close. There was still no room for complacency. What if I was forced to call for a resupply? What if we were closed in by a storm?

Elaine came in loud and clear on the radio that night. She told us two Twin Otters had been hired to pick us up. I was mad as hell. I had arranged before we left England that our pick-up 'plane would be capable of carrying our friends from the States as well as us. I made Jock get hold of the Base Manager. I felt our sponsors were being screwed and I didn't like it.

Hugh shouted over, "We have a choice. Tea or tea to drink followed by mutton or mutton, and even though I was desperately hungry, and his cooking was superb, I was nearly gagging on the food.

Mitch fired up the Trimble. "Eight miles travelled today, lads."

"This is going to be a close run thing, Mitch," I said. "If we make it, I'll treat you to a loaf of bread at Narwhal's."

Day 17 – Mitch's Journal

We are now into the final stage of our journey. Less than forty miles to the Pole and four days' supply of rations, we felt confident of success. A confidence that began to fade when we saw the terrain in the Basin. We were expecting some pressure

177

ridges and boulder ice as we moved on to the open sea, but nothing like that which was now set before us. We moved to the edge and prepared to assault the final stage. Now the true size of the boulder ridges was brought home to us. In places they were stacked over twenty feet high, but it was the sheer density that would slow us down. The paulks, which had performed so well for us thus far, now acted like anchors, making us wish we had given more serious consideration to the option of carrying rucksacks to meet such an eventuality. Every gap between adjacent boulders threatened to pull the sledges off the required route, snag them, or merely topple them, making them impossible to pull. Skis, that had proved so valuable earlier in the route, were now riding redundant on the top of sledges, and caught on the ice debris at every bend or change of direction. With most of the food now consumed it became difficult to pack the sledges with a low centre of gravity, with the result they were much more prone to topple, which they did with monotonous regularity. Walking forward was difficult, but climbing back over the ice to right a sledge every twenty paces was exhausting. Every now and then a section of flat ice would appear; sometimes for just a few hundred feet. At other times we would enjoy the almost forgotten luxury of walking on flat ground for an hour or so, but each time the pressure ridges would return to haunt us, making us fight for every mile. The risk of broken legs or sprained ankles now became very real as we stumbled on, suffering the effects of fatigue, terrain and the weight of our sledges. Snow-covered boulders hid a myriad of holes and cracks we could not possibly hope to avoid. The lead man tended to find the majority, but there was always a surprise or two waiting for the remaining four.

When evening came I dreaded checking the GPS; announcing a mere eight mile gain after climbing through the ice for ten hours; this was met with silence from the team. They seemed to think I must have made a mistake and began to doubt the accuracy of the GPS. Whatever they thought, it did nothing to cheer them up. With less than thirty miles to go, and only three days' rations remaining, genuine doubts began to set in as to whether we could complete the journey without resupply, which would deny us the record of first unsupported team. We tried to cut rations but were now increasing our march times each day and required more food, not less. Eventually we settled for no change in ration issue and hoped for the best. In attempting to stifle my hunger pains I tried to eat my emergency candle, which, being made of animal fat, is supposed to be edible. If it hadn't been so hard I might have eaten more! As it was I could only manage about three quarters of an inch before having to give up. The cold had already cost me two teeth, shattered on pieces of chocolate. I did not want to lose any more. I continued to feel desperately hungry. By now we were getting close enough to the Pole to require us to march on an accurate bearing and plot our position regularly on a graph with GPS updates to adjust our heading. I found it amazing that despite using some of the best and most expensive satellite tracking systems available today, plus a very expensive compass, we were adjusting our position and bearing every hour, using a protractor, the sun, a pencil held vertically to cast a shadow and a set of sun tables!

We could no longer afford to take the easiest route East, as deviations from our headings now would be critical in reaching the final position. This often meant ignoring easier routes to our left and right. We had to walk directly towards the Pole.

Day 17 – Hugh's Journal

We moved into the rubble last night and at that time decided to tackle this problem with a fresh body in the morning. Talk last night was of home and the pick-up, revealing a great wish to be away from this inhospitable land. The 21st April will go down in my mind as one of the hardest and most demoralising of my life. We started well and as luck would have it, were moving out to the Basin, albeit South. However, it began to become more obvious that this rubble was not a small band. Every opportunity that presented itself we climbed a berg and attempted to see a route through, or at least an end, but to no avail. The rubble finally closed in at 1.00 p.m. and from that time movement was extremely slow. We walked over terrain that was broken slabs of ice the size of a car, covered by deep snow. Each step would take you in up to your waist. Although now considerably lighter, the paulks were constantly turning over and almost required carrying at some points. As each trail breaker flagged someone went forward to take his place. The hourly stops became meetings of very tired men, sharing a brew and a few biscuits. Thus we continued until 4.30 p.m. when Neill once again took the lead. He saw an open pan to the left. As we broke through, it could be seen to be connected to another pan. A small ride allowed us to observe forward and to be rewarded with the sight of a "flat" vista! Much celebration was heard at that point. I am slightly more circumspect and adopt a more "take it as it comes" attitude. We pitched camp and food was increased by one man ration to replace the calories we had lost that day. There is an air of achievement about the camp tonight – not for what we are about to do, but for the simple hard day's work of men who had travelled eight miles in terrain over which others made only three.

Day 17 – Neill's Journal

I've been to hell and back today, crying on the inside for Lindsey, Christian and Ashley, and on the surface in pain. For the first time my body said, "that's it" but somehow I pulled through. The multi-year ice became a vicious unrelenting obstacle for most of the day. Mitch thinks it could run all the way to the Pole because of last year's freak conditions. Just when all seemed to be losing faith, it was time to swap the lead with Jock and pick up the route. The first thirty minutes were as the rest of the day: struggling, falling, lifting, falling again, getting absolutely nowhere. Then I received my good fortune. I found a gap – is this my good fortune for sticking it? We broke on to an ice pan and from a high vantage point more openings appeared, and at last we started to gain ground. We ended up with eight and a half miles, and with no evidence that conditions will change. Jock still talks of doing eighteen to twenty miles a day! We have all fallen into the trap. This place dominates, each day must be taken as a separate challenge. In this company anything is possible. "Billy the Bag" is now well in front in the

World Series with Hugh, I'm sure my bag is female. Jock didn't sleep again for all but nine hours.

DAY 18 – Wednesday 22nd April

I pulled out the Douglas protractor and Nautical Almanac. Derek Waters had worked out the figures for the team before we arrived in Canada. "This is a sun compass," I said. "Right now, that's North, that's South, and the Pole's in that direction, with the sun shadow to your left. Mitch and I will double check each hour and give you an updated shadow. Neill, you're in front the whole of today. Hugh, back him up."

It seemed much colder today, especially on our faces and hands. The Bach was now well behind us, and nearly out of sight, but the mountains to the North could still be seen, with the sun shining on them. Neill got straight into a flat pan of ice and our hearts soared. "Neill, you're going a little to the South." "Neill, you're going a little to the West." Hugh felt it better to go in any direction as long as we kept on flat ground and made gradual progress forwards. Each hour we gave an updated position. I was starting to get brassed off. We had come too far to screw this up. We had walked North, South, East, and West in a huge zig-zag. An hour before the end of the day, I just couldn't stand it any more.

"Hugh, for Christ's sake, we're going in completely the wrong direction!"

I was stunned by his reply. "You go your way, and we'll go ours and we'll meet you at the Pole."

Had I been younger, I would probably have thumped him. Alicia had taught me a little patience. I counted to ten. We would be stopping in thirty minutes' time anyway.

We were all totally shattered, and I put Hugh's comments down to the fact that he was so tired. When we camped, he forgot about digging the tents in. We just plonked them down and crawled in exhausted.

I said to Hugh, "OK, by zig-zagging all day, how many miles do you think we went?"

"Definitely our best day," he answered, "twenty-two miles."

I asked Neill.

"Twenty."

Then Jock.

"Twenty-four, and nearly at the Pole."

Then Mitch.

"Twelve miles."

"Rubbish, never. Rubbish," from the cook tent.

"I think eight miles," I said.

It suddenly dawned on the other tent that we were serious.

"What's the Trimble say?" they all bellowed.

"I'm waiting for it to warm up," Mitch replied.

After ten minutes, "OK, we have travelled the grand distance of eleven miles."

Not a word from the other tent.

Later, I spoke with Hugh privately. "Hugh, I'm telling you now, you either follow the sun compass tomorrow, or we get picked up tonight."

It was a few moments before he answered, then, "I'm sorry. I was well out of order."

We had eighteen miles to go, with two days' supply of food left. What if it took us another four days? I started to make a list for a resupply flight. The last item on the list was oranges. I was desperate for an orange.

Elaine came in on the radio, "Sorry, you guys, no pick-up for Thursday. We have a problem getting a 'plane. It will have to be Friday."

Jock did his crust. He wanted to go home now. We all did. Actually, facing the fact that the 'plane was unavailable until Friday gave us a more realistic view of our situation. We were never going to achieve eighteen miles in one day coping with these conditions. Jock was having none of it. He wanted to talk to the pilot, but he wasn't around. "Who's the owner? Where is he?"

"He's not around either."

Neill and Hugh gradually placated him.

Elaine told us the pick-up would now be with one aircraft, as originally agreed.

When we got into our tent Mitch immediately organised himself. One pile of clothes was for the next day, the other pile to go into the paulk. A third pile would be for that night. I was the opposite, being a total slob, and it showed – "Mitch, have you seen my pencil?" "Mitch, have you got my gloves?" "Mitch, some swine has nicked my watch."

He jumped over my bag. "Quick! Quick! I can see a thief running over there!"

We had been in some tight situations before, but this was the closest. We knew each other extremely well. Each night one of the lads would shout, "Scoff!" I would grab my bowlful. Handing it to Mitch I would turn and grab his bowl. During the last few days, I was damn sure that when my back was turned to take the second bowl, Mitch had swiped a couple of spoonfuls of my grub. "Did you just nick a spoonful?" He would grin and shake his head. "Open your mouth, you sod."

Day 18 – Hugh's Journal

I wrote this journal the following morning – yesterday was as hard as the previous one but less rewarding. We started quite well and soon found a number of largish pans, but we had strayed South, and it seemed we were being forced South by the ice. After the first hour Neill took the lead – it almost seemed as if he was gifted with knowledge of pans! We were now moving from pan to pan, and even through rubble the route was good. We appeared to be making good progress in the direction of the Pole – at one point a very large pan took two and a half hours to cross. We moved off it at 6.00 p.m. into another band of rubble, which was thick, and appeared to have few routes through. All of the group were tired so we pitched camp to get rested in preparation for what seemed to be yet another obstacle. I felt sure we must have travelled twenty-three to twenty-four miles in the right direction, but when we turned the Trimble on, to the utter disbelief of the crew, we had only gone eleven miles in the right direction – too few for so far.

"Well, lads, one way or another, it's getting close," I said. "Eighteen miles to go. The more we do today, the less tomorrow."

For the first time our breakfast was horrible, a mixture of oats and left-overs from the monster bags. We could see no mountains that day. Neill was out in front. After ten minutes we were going South.

"Stop," I said. "Today we are going straight on this bearing, plus or minus fifty foot detours. We must stick to it."

Each hour, we checked the figures and double-checked the direction. I didn't want to end up going in the wrong direction again. Once again, dark clouds were visible in the South, probably above open water. Neill made an unscheduled stop. He was having trouble with his backside. Hugh gave him TCP. I told him to stuff something between his cheeks. Off he went again. He was like a Roman Gladiator, throwing a javelin into the far distance, with the rest of the team hastening to retrieve it.

The pace was good all day. We had learned to pull our sledges through the smallest of restrictions, and we could now gauge a gap to five millimetres each side. Neill managed to find a couple of pans of ice. It had been the flattest ground we had seen for some time. My mind was now thinking ahead. We would need a good ice pan for the pick-up. What if we didn't find one? It was a question already asked by every member of the team. Actually, I was hoping, as a last resort, that the 'plane would find a pan on which to land, and we would walk to it.

Keeping strictly to our bearing, we felt we were making good progress. We were now traversing flattish pans, but none of us dared ask how well we were doing. The excitement and tension was growing.

It was a shattered crew that gathered to make camp that night after Neill slowly came to a halt. Both Mitch and I were limping, Jock and Hugh stumbled in, bringing up the rear. Our spirits were flagging and bodies were falling apart.

All five of us huddled into the cold tent – not so cold now, as the temperature had risen to -15°C. Mitch was in his maggot warming up batteries for the Trimble. We were all hovering around like schoolboys. I secretly prayed, "Please help us, give us some distance."

"OK, waypoint Tango to waypoint X-ray, we have the grand total of . . . "

"Come on, come on!"

"Seven miles to go."

"Yeah! Yeah! Yeah!"

We all shook hands. "Jock," I said, "call up the 'plane for tomorrow night. I want the pick-up late, about 7.00 p.m. just in case we have problems. If we start at seven in the morning, that will give us twelve hours to do seven miles. We've never had a day where we've covered less than seven miles. Have them come in on latitude line seventy-nine degrees twelve minutes North. They'll find us either on the Pole or along that latitude line. They should bring in emergency food and fuel for us in case they are unable to land."

Jock relayed it all to Elaine. "Can you repeat that back to me, Elaine?"

Elaine had the pilot next to the radio. "Confirmed, pick-up at 7.00 p.m. tomorrow."

We could hardly believe it. "Jock, tell her we want pizza, doughnuts, apples, beer, and roast beef sandwiches."

Seven miles to go. My mind was working overtime. "What if they don't find us? What if there's open water? What if we break a leg?" Given the wrong sort of luck, seven miles is a long way. The food was now a mish-mash of left-overs from other meals, but it was all we had. An air of excitement fell over the camp that night. So close!

Day 19 – Hugh's Journal

Yesterday was a day of distance in the wrong direction. Today would be less of a compromise to the easy route – nothing worth having comes easy. However, I was still of a mind to make some compromise as the thought of breaking through miles of barriers was mindless. Kim and I had a disagreement. I was in the wrong. There are obstacles such as pride and conceit in our mind which are far greater than those of a physical nature. In the end I followed Neill's sense of right and did my best to help him. He twisted and turned, and once more found open pans, albeit less frequently than yesterday. It took four and a half hours to make three and a half miles, but at least it was forward to our goal. We are now extending the work periods to one and a half hours, causing me some concern that with only 3 lt/g for the whole day, we might be stretching our bodies to the limit. We seem to be perspiring less, there is less evidence of this on the outside of our jackets. Our urine seems to be yellow which would indicate everything is OK but with trg values at six litres per man per day it would seem to be very low. On these intakes we are existing quite happily on one litre of water. We pitched camp and the Trimble was fired up. We have seven miles to go to enter the area of the Pole. The 'plane has been called for 7.00 p.m. tomorrow. We must make good progress.

I love my wife, and look forward to our meeting. I have tried my best, and with the Grace of God, may yet achieve what I set out to do.

Day 19 – Neill's Journal

Today I have to find a path with the support of Hugh, who is, as ever, guiding me and preventing me making too many mistakes. We slog for three and a half hours and gain only three and a half miles. This time I cried on the outside, fortunately my sun glasses prevented the rest of the team being aware of my distress. Although every part of me hurt, the tears were really due to missing my family and the sheer frustration at not being able to get past this wall. The afternoon was better, we make better progress and end up almost ten miles nearer the Pole. No one can ever take this away from me. It is the greatest achievement of my life. I hope Lindsey will believe that she is married to someone a bit different in their make up, that she will be proud of me, and some day my children will understand and be proud of their father. Perhaps my dad will be proud of me, who knows. Must admit to being a little worried about work, and Lindsey having to cope by herself. I keep thinking about her grandfather, I have to let him know he has been with me every day.

I'll remember these days as some of the hardest of my life. Once again I had to melt the ice on my boots – I was so fearful that if they got so frozen one day I might not get them off, or, more importantly, might not be able to get them back on again. Neil led and this time, although we were still slow tacking bearings from pan to pan, we were more positive about the direction we were taking. Kim giving a lot of good advice. What amazes me is how little liquid we are managing to survive on now that we have reduced the work periods to an hour and a half. It is so hard now that I can't even think of my favourite thoughts – my little boy and girl, and my wife. It will be nice to see Debbie again and have a good argument, but there is no way I am going to give up on this one. We are going to get there even if we have to crawl there. I may have been frustrated with the pace but in comparison with my fellow Durhamite, Robert Swan, and his last trip to the Arctic, we are really sprinting. In similar conditions their team had been lucky to achieve one and a half miles a day fighting through this rubble, but here we were doing nine, ten, twelve miles a day, quite extraordinary. Kim has arranged to call the 'plane in for Friday at 7.00. I think this would give us a realistic chance of achieving our goal before we run out of food. In any case I made my feelings known that even if we have to walk through the night we are going to get there. I am determined to get back for my mother's medal ceremony in Scotland, and Kim could see that there would be very little that could persuade me otherwise. I must also confess that I have a different view to the rest of the team as far as achieving our goal is concerned. To me this is wholly a team effort. In my view my job has already been done in keeping the pace up in the early stages. This effort I know has exhausted me and I am now on empty – just my own determination making sure I keep going, so in my view it would be perfectly acceptable if a couple of members of the team with backpacks go forward to achieve our goal, which is, of course, to be the first to the Geomagnetic Pole. I would be quite content in my own mind that we as a group achieve our objective in which case I would vote for Kim and Mitch to be the ones to make the Pole. However, as far as Kim is concerned it is all or none, so on we trudge.

Tonight we know we are very close – only about seven miles to go. We are all determined to make an early start tomorrow, the aim being to be away at seven-thirty in the morning.

CHAPTER TEN

TO THE POLE

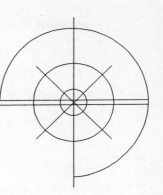

DAY 20 – Friday 24th April

As we wished to get an early start, Hugh had already prepared breakfast and the flasks. Apart from cat-napping, sleep was denied me last night. In fact, the occupants of both tents were restless. This would hopefully be my last night's sleep in a tent for some time to come.

Suddenly I awoke with a jolt. "Jock, Jock, what's the time?"

"For Christ's sake calm down. It's only two in the morning."

Three times during the night I woke with the impression we had overslept.

Hugh fared less well than the rest of us, being the only one without kids. The rest of us had learned to catch sleep between cries for bottles, etc. This trip has changed Hugh – before, he'd seen it all, done it all and been everywhere, I think the Arctic had humbled him like everyone else, and he had become a more mature person.

During my waking hours, I retraced the events of each consecutive day from the start of our walk at Eureka. Summing up our present physical state it seemed to me that it equalled Wally Herbert's condition when he arrived at Eureka. There were many reasons why I would remember this expedition. The beauty and majesty of the mountains, the team work, the hardships, the humour, but above all

Pack ice in the Kane Basin. The Bache Peninsular behind us.

Five contented men. The Pole itself. (UN Flag).

the spirit of care and concern each person had shown for the other team members. When we were fatigued or despondent harsh words were sometimes spoken but they were quickly forgotten. Having brought five very different men together, all with strong ideas and dominant personalities, I would have expected some major wars. In the event nothing like that occurred. Each had complimented the other. If I was down, someone on the up-beat would lift my spirits. When someone was faltering we clucked around like mother hens to help. Camaraderie is a term that is often used loosely. Having undertaken many expeditions, this one, above all, personified it.

"Jock, Jock, what's the time?"

"Six o'clock".

"OK, OK, we're moving."

Everyone stirred slowly. Hugh passed the breakfast through. It was the last of our breakfast food. All that remained was one monster bag to eat during the day, and one main meal. That was the sum total of our food. Hugh had prepared forty main breakfasts and dinners, aided by Neill and Jock. With the notable exception of this morning, he had surpassed himself. He presented us with a concoction conjured up from a mixture of all our left-overs. I ate a few mouthfuls, but gagged. How on earth could I tell him? Fortunately I was saved by Jock saying, "Hugh, I really am sorry, but I just can't eat this." As luck would have it, Hugh couldn't see into our tent. We poured the gunge into a plastic bag and put it in our pockets – just in case we needed it in an emergency.

Mitch shouted, "Jock, you ungrateful swine, how could you not eat that?"

"I know, I know. I'm sorry."

Little time was lost in packing up our sledges. They were all lightweight now. It was 8.00 a.m., our earliest start. The lads all gathered around me as if it were a council of war.

"When we started, I said, 'One for all, and all for one'. We have really lived up to this. Eleven hours to do seven miles. But don't get complacent. We can still cancel the 'plane up to 4.00 p.m. If by 4.00 p.m. we know we won't make it I will order a resupply and not a pick-up. So let's not sell ourselves short."

Neill harnessed up his sledge and moved off at a run. Fifteen minutes later he was still going at a tremendous pace. After thirty minutes disaster struck. Neill's sledge split in two. Of all the days for this to happen, fate had chosen this one! Mitch pulled his tool kit out and got straight down to it. He drilled holes on either side of the split and used helicopter plastic ties to hold it together. If it didn't work we decided we would split the load, and ditch the sledge. Neill's load consisted only of his personal kit. Within fifteen minutes the repair was completed. Neill was off again. Each hour he asked for a sun shadow, and then was away again.

I asked Mitch and Hugh if I could borrow one of their tooth brushes – I hadn't brought one with me on the trip.

"No way," they said.

"I'll give you ten pounds for it."

"No."

"Twenty pounds?"

"No."

"Fifty pounds?"

"No. I'll let you use it if you don't swear all day."

A tall order.

By now we were flying through the rubble. After three and a half hours we stopped. Mitch had been walking with the Trimble down his front to keep it fully operative. As soon as we stopped, one of us unhitched his paulk, whilst someone else laid a thermal mat on the ice on which Mitch stretched out. This allowed him to keep the Trimble warm inside his jacket, keep the aerial vertical, and at the same time read the display. The total operation only took a few seconds but it seemed like hours.

"Well, what does it say?"

Mitch smiled. "Three miles done."

He worked out how many miles to the Pole and what direction to take. We kept going.

"Go, go, go."

Jock was getting frustrated with his paulk. He started to kick it.

"Jock, that sledge has been through thick and thin!"

"Sorry, sledge."

The pack ice wasn't any easier, but we all felt "this was the day". For a while, our aches and pains were forgotten. We stopped after another three hours. Again Mitch was on his back.

"What a sight! Two more miles done."

It was getting close. We had only once come across a possible landing site in the last six and a half hours, and that proved to be too short. My mind was starting to work in overdrive. Would we have to keep going to Greenland to get picked up? I decided to keep this gruesome thought to myself.

Neill moved off again. My stomach was rumbling like mad. I

could almost smell those beef sandwiches. After two hours, Mitch was on his back. A large grin spread across his face. "Point seven miles to go, directly North-east."

"Yeah! Oh boy!"

We were all yelping like men possessed. After thirty minutes we broke into the biggest flat pan of ice we had come across on our entire crossing of the Kane Basin. Someone was looking out for us! We quickly made it to the middle. It was the only pan we had found which was suitable to put an aircraft down on. It looked at least a mile across in every direction. The ice was well consolidated, so we decided to leave the sledges, take our warm kit, cameras, flag and rifle and follow Mitch, who now had the Trimble on full time. Mitch and Neill, who were in the lead, stopped. Mitch drew a line in the snow. That was it! Handshakes all around.

For a time, no one spoke. It was difficult to define the expression on our faces as we had our glasses on, but a few tears rolled down the cheeks of several of us.

"Two hundred and seventy-six miles in twenty days. Thank you all," I said.

"Awesome. Hardest thing I ever did."

Hugh then handed me his tooth brush. Neill still couldn't speak.

Jock said, "Don't ever ask me again to join you on a holiday which is supposed to be a walk in the park."

Mitch said he had been hungry from the hour the expedition started and that I should reimburse him for the amount of doughnuts he was going to eat.

Jock got the flag out and Mitch determined which direction was facing London. Jock marshalled us into a line. Slowly the words crept out: "God save our gracious Queen . . . " We all stood bolt upright, and sang the whole national anthem. Who said patriotism was dead? – we all knew the anthem word for word.

In the midst of all this euphoria it suddenly dawned on us that we had better get back to the sledges and make ready for the pick-up. Slowly we retraced our steps, a little reluctant to leave this desolate spot on the globe we had fought so hard to reach. On the way back, Mitch said sheepishly, "I have something to tell you. You know those hand-warmers that you threw out on the first day as rubbish, because they didn't get warm? Well they did. I picked up the one you threw away and after ten minutes, I nearly burned my hand. Each night I would put a new warmer in the bottom of my bag and my feet were as warm as toast. That will teach you to hang on for a couple of minutes to see if something works."

I told everyone to set the radio up, erect one tent only, and to keep the paulks packed in case we had to move. "And keep the flares and signal mirror handy."

Mitch would now be in charge of the radio communication with the pilot. We walked around the pan to see if we could see a suitable strip. At the sound of an engine I looked to see a huge orange bird come into view. I was stunned. They were an hour early. The aircraft circled and circled, obviously the pilot didn't like our pan. We ran back. "Take the tent down," I shouted. Mitch got on the radio. It seemed the pilot considered the pan to be too bumpy.

The 'plane continued to circle round for twenty minutes. "Please, please land," I thought. I knew if they landed, we would be out tonight. If they couldn't they would drop food, give us co-ordinates to walk to, and pick us up later.

We waited with what patience we could muster, watching the 'plane orbiting our position. Finally, the welcome words came over the radio from the pilot. "OK British Mobile, we have a flat lead point five miles North of you. We will try and land."

Mitch talked his pilot jargon back. "Zero five miles or five miles? Confirm."

"British Mobile that is zero point five."

Mitch shouted for us to keep a bearing on its flight path in case we lost sight of it when it landed. Gradually the aircraft descended lower and lower. I prayed for it to land. The roar of reverse thrust told us the pilot had decided it was safe to land.

We quickly packed the radio into a sledge and set off in the direction of the 'plane, retracing our earlier steps. We could just see the tip of the tailplane above the ice rubble. It took us thirty minutes to get to where we had previously been standing and there, over an ice ridge, fifty yards from the Pole, stood the aircraft. I could see Jim and Elaine. Someone else was walking towards us. "Hi! I'm Jeff May, Jim May's son." It had not been possible to include other members of the party from the States on the flight. There had been no guarantee that we would be found and the extra weight would have consumed fuel which might be needed to conduct a search. As it turned out the experienced pilots said it had been the most accurate and best pick-up they had ever made. The Trimble reading on the 'plane matched ours exactly.

It was wonderful seeing Jim again, we owed everything to him. Eating, drinking, photographs and filming all passed into a blur.

Walking to the plane.

Eating and drinking at the Pole.

With the May Family.

Boarding the Twin Otter at the Pole.

At the crack of dawn – or at least that is what it feels like, in a place where the sun shines for twenty-four hours – everyone was up. With only seven miles to go we were determined (although by no means certain) that this day would see us at the Pole, with a pick-up 'plane waiting for us. ENDEX fever, as we in the Army know it, was in the air and moods had changed – for better and worse! Although we had only twenty-four hours' rations left, Hugh decided to give us a slap up breakfast, and poured in everything he could find, to build our energy levels for the final sprint. How was he to know that in the other tent, Kim and I had been dreaming of fried eggs and bacon? When the unusually full bowls were passed into our tent, even I, who just three days before had tried to eat my emergency candle, had trouble eating it at all. Kim, who had his sights set on the contents of a hamper in the pick-up 'plane, and was prepared to starve for a day, decided he would go without. This left him faced with the dilemma of returning the bowl without upsetting the Chef. After scouring the tent for suitable disposal methods the "breakfast" was eventually deposited into a polythene bag. The congealed mass froze solid within minutes and was put in his pocket – just in case.

Kim got a bit agitated with Jock, Neill and Hugh for taking so long in breaking camp, but he soon calmed down as we made off. We seemed to take an age before we got any rhythm going, and after numerous halts for "picky" little things, which wasted much time, we had just found our stride, when Neill, who was at the front, stopped suddenly, with a sledge that looked as though it was at the end of its tether. There was a split, almost the entire length of his sledge, which met another, running at right-angles. The contents would soon be spread across the Arctic floor. Desperate to keep the momentum going, Jock and I set about repairing the sledge by stitching it with "Tyraps". Within ten minutes the repair was completed. It remains in my memory for two reasons: despite stopping regularly to warm my hands in Neill's coat I suffered for months afterwards with frostnip, and secondly, having been scorned by Kim for taking additional weight, in the form of my tool kit. I was able to give him my best ever "I told you so!" look of smugness on the completion of the job. The drudgery continued relentlessly. Boulder ice seemed to topple the sledges at every opportunity and Jock, in a pique of frustration, set about it with his ski pole. I couldn't help but chuckle inwardly as this bastion of patience and good humour started to shout at his sledge as if it were a rebel Labrador puppy in need of obedience lessons.

Day 20 – Neill's Journal

Very early start, absolutely vital to give us any chance of getting to the Pole before the 'plane arrives. Within an hour of starting out, with the going as hard as ever over the rubble, my paulk got to the point of no return! Mitch repaired it with no fuss in under ten minutes, he is so practical and unflappable. Using just a penknife to make holes, he sewed the hull together with plastic strips. From then on I had virtually to carry and lower the paulk to avoid any more damage.

Morning progresses and we check direction and distance with the Trimble. Desperately forging ahead with Hugh, trying not to lose forward direction. Gaps start to appear – it is enough.

Trimble double checked and we are only point seven of a mile short of our target! Route North, both Mitch and I had already picked a path North into the open pan. Excitement builds, paulks are left in the middle of an open pan, and we walk, with no equipment other than the Trimble and cameras. Mitch once again checks the Trimble and nearly crushes my hand – time 5.14 p.m. Resolute time, 10.14 GMT. WE ARE THERE! Unbelievable emotion, but no one shouts. Sang "God Save The Queen". Photos with the united shirt, school flag – felt so proud, and so unbelievably lucky to be with the boys. Back to the paulks to set up ready for the 'plane, and then a dream is complete.

With Kim and Mitch looking for a landing strip, one tent is put up, and Hugh, Jock and myself set up the radio. A brilliant orange bird appears and flies over our heads. Kim flips out! Everyone tries to calm him, and we pack up the gear. We are in contact with the 'plane. The pilot tells us to watch his flight path, and lands on the spot where we had been celebrating a short time before. We virtually run to meet them – champagne, photos. The Pilot said it is the most accurate pick-up he has ever had. His Trimble exactly matches ours!

At this point I don't know why I have done this thing, but it was brilliant, even the bits that hurt.

As Mitch and I pack the radio we hear a wolf calling. Was

it the Arctic saying Farewell?

Day 20 – Jock's Journal

The main problem for us last night was that Kim's excitement was a realisation of a ten-year dream. Consequently I was woken up at one, two, three o'clock in the morning by Kim who did not seem to be aware of the time, thinking that we were all sleeping in. I kept on telling him what the time was and to go back to sleep, though of course the only person he was waking up was myself. It was impossible to get annoyed with him – he was just infected by the excitement and this moment of history, I suppose, because, yes, that's what we were doing – we were creating our own little bit of history.

Hugh woke up with a wild gleam in his eyes and he was determined to make the most of the moment as far as breakfast was concerned and literally everything we had left was thrown into the pot. If we did not make it that day we would be surviving on air, I'm afraid. The problem was that the combination of oats, biscuits and muesli, on our shrunken stomachs was rather hard to take. Not wanting to upset Hugh, I manfully stuffed spoon after spoon of this vile concoction of his down my throat till in the end it was just becoming too much for me and I made a suggestion to Hugh that I was really a bit full now and had had quite enough, to which came a chorus of voices from the other tent saying, no really I must eat this all up, and that it was good for me, and that they had all finished theirs, and that they didn't want me to be a liability on the last day. Nevertheless the effort was really too much and I had to leave quite a bit of it. Of course, what I was not to know was that in the other tent Kim and Mitch had also not been able to face it and had ditched theirs, but the joke was really on me, though Hugh did not want to say anything to me at the time because really every other meal he had done was quite a culinary miracle. This meal really was like having a lead brick in your stomach. As you can imagine starting off that morning, I was not in exactly the best frame of minds. Nevertheless as the day wore on I started to feel a bit better.

Our first problem of the day was Neill's paulk which had been the paulk taken by Kim to the Magnetic Pole and this finally gave up the ghost and started splitting in two. Fortunately Mitch was carrying with him some plastic cable telephone ties so he and I drilled some holes in it and quite literally stitched the paulk back together again. Believe me, that's one item of equipment I'm going to take with me wherever I go from now on.

We are now getting very close – maybe half hour. Mitch, who is our chief navigator, would stop and stick the global position system GPS down next to his balls and warm it up enough to be able to get a reading. Goodness knows what that must have done for his sex life, but as he already has three daughters I presume he is not going to be trying again. Anyway, it did wonders for our positioning. We steadily moved towards our goal and the last seven miles crept slowly by.

We are actually making quite good pace. We came across several flat pans of ice going in the right direction so we were making good time. About half past four we came to a flat pan of ice and the GPS showed that we are very close to the Pole. The decision was made to leave the paulks where they were and to walk forward to the Pole which we reckoned was about half a mile away. I had gone twenty yards when I suddenly remembered the rifle and rushed back to pick it up. I was not going to be surprised by a polar bear in our moment of glory. Well we found this hump which was the Pole and we stood around and congratulated each other and shook hands and generally behaved like a bunch of school boys. We weren't quite sure what to do so we turned round to the general direction of London and sang "God Save the Queen". We then walked back to the paulks and were just erecting the tent when, an hour earlier than planned, the Twin Otter flew over head at about twenty feet above us. We frantically tried to get the radio into operation, and hoped that they would land quite close to us. Kim again got quite excited about this because I think he could see his taxi home disappearing over the horizon, I don't think he was in the mood to walk a long way to a pick-up for the flight back. Fortunately for us they in fact landed about half a mile away, in fact right damn smack back on top of the Pole so we walked back to the Twin Otter to be met by Elaine, Jim and Jeff and I can tell you they were a very welcome sight indeed.

DAY 20 – Going Home

Within a short space of time we were skimming along the ice and off. The Arctic ice that had been our home for the past twenty days now passed by thousands of feet below us in the pale red light of early dusk.

For the first time in many days our well-being was in the hands of someone else. We all looked out of the window, gazing at beautiful mountains to the North. Viewed from this altitude the sea ice that had seemed so insurmountable to us looked smooth and lovely. We headed across the Basin, where strips of open water were dotted around, then to Cape Camperdown. The open water was now lapping the shores of the Bach Peninsula. It truly had been a race against time.

Relaxing in the aircraft seat I opened my diary and started to jot down modifications for the next expedition. However carefully these trips are planned, experience does not always match theory and you come to realise that better decisions could have been made.

I wrote notes to remind me of changes I would wish to see in equipment, supplies, navigation, etc. However, when it came to assessing the team, I wrote but one word. "Perfect!"

APPENDIX ONE

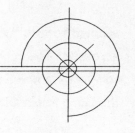

NAVIGATION
BY CAPTAIN RICHARD MITCHELL

For the expedition we were all allocated individual areas of responsibility, mine was navigation. As an Army helicopter pilot I had both a professional and personal interest in the topic. In addition I had worked extensively with the Global Positioning System (GPS). Here I have attempted to explain in more detail the important aspects of the subject, as I found them.

First among the problems of navigation in the Arctic is the position of the Magnetic Pole and its effect on the compass. Currently it is in a position in the vicinity of Lougheed Island (77 degrees 30 minutes North, 105 degrees West). This meant that at the start of our journey our compass pointed almost due West! The magnetic field is also very weak, which makes any readings highly susceptible to metallic objects, and the compass needle takes a long time to settle. Our compass was a high quality oil-filled device made by Sunto (similar to the standard Silva) but incorporated a declination ring. This allowed us to pre-set the magnetic declination for the region which in the Kane Basin was 72 degrees West. I had taken the compass as a back-up but anticipated using the GPS in order to calculate the heading required to take us to the Pole and a sun compass to establish that heading. In the event this proved to be an easily workable and time-efficient method of route finding although it is interesting to note that with all the technology now available to expeditions, we were relying upon the oldest reference known to man – the sun! The principle behind the sun compass is quite elementary. As most boy scouts will know, provided that you can see the sun and you know the time of day, the position of South (and therefore True North) can be calculated. We used exactly the same principle but carried a set of solar tables so as to be able to work more accurately and compensate for time zone changes. In order to calculate the heading required for each leg of the march we used a pencil (which cast a shadow) held vertically in the centre of a Douglas protractor to indicate the North/South line; the lead man then used the pencil and the periphery of the protractor as a sight to pick a reference on a distant object on the required heading, and marched towards it. Once under way it was simply a matter of keeping one's own shadow relative to the body, as a reference, in order to ensure that we stayed on track. We repeated this process each hour to allow for the 15 degrees movement of the sun in that time. Of course, such a method relies on being able to see the sun! We were indeed lucky to have good enough weather throughout to make this system workable, but would have had to resort to the compass in the event of poor weather.

Throughout the journey we used a standard nautical chart of the area on 1:250 000 scale for route finding. This chart was overlaid with both Latitude and Longitude and the world-wide Military Grid. We had decided to duplicate the navigation "effort" as much as possible by taking as many different systems as possible should any one fail.

Firstly, we would be navigating around a charted land mass for nearly all of the expedition so we could use the map directly. Secondly we took two seaport GPS systems; these were the Magellan and the Trimble, which many Gulf veterans will be familiar with. Finally we used the relatively new Argos system. The complete Argos package weighs about three pounds, measures 7 x 6 x 16 cm with a small whip antenna and runs on sealed lithium batteries which are reported to last sixty days. The system operates through transit satellites which, as they pass overhead, interrogate the Argos, determine its position and collect any data transmitted. The satellite then downloads the data to a ground station where it can be accessed via computer and relayed to the base crew. The data which can be transmitted by this system is in the form of a four digit binary code which would be set by the team using four toggle switches prior to switching on each day and would be in the form of a pre-arranged code for our base camp. For example, most evenings, we would select the switch array to indicate the code 0001 which, when received by our base crew, told them that all was well. It therefore becomes possible to send a total of sixteen different messages using this system. In addition to the four data switches there is a fifth emergency switch which will alert staff at the Argos centre who would in turn warn the relevant authorities. The codes that we adopted are listed below:

0001 All is well.

0010 Slow going – poor weather.

0011 Slow going – poor terrain.

0100 No movement – poor weather.

0101 No movement – poor terrain.

0110 Need resupply – food (no emergency).

0111 Need resupply – equipment (no emergency).

1000 Need evacuation – no emergency.

1001 Need evacuation – emergency.

1010	Open water.
1011	Polar bear attack.
1100	Have weather suitable for aircraft.
1101	Have ice pan suitable for landing.
1110	Left vacant.
1111	Left vacant.
0000	Left vacant.

This system, although very useful, has obvious limitations. Since the data is received by the base crew it is only possible to get a position report by radio. Since the system has to be left on for four hours to get a fix we were switching it on in the evening and having to wait until the next radio schedule to get the information. For us that meant the following evening which then meant the information was twenty-four hours old and told us where we were the night before!

As a real-time position fixing system therefore, we opted for two GPS systems. A sextant was considered but the bulk and dependency upon a good sun shot coupled with previous experience with GPS systems persuaded me to opt for the latter. We took the Magellan system as a back-up to the Trimble but fortunately never had to use it. I found the Magellan much more cumbersome to use and the time taken to "collect" the three satellites necessary for a "fix" excessive. The Trimble in contrast however was much more user friendly. Having had a fair amount of experience with this system I am probably a little biased, however a fix with the Trimble never took more than sixty seconds, and compares favourably with the Magellan which on a couple of occasions took in excess of eight minutes; standing around in temperatures of minus 40°C makes one appreciative of the time saving.

The actual position of the Pole was calculated for the expedition by the British Geological Society and was given as 79 degrees 12 minutes North, 71 degrees 12 minutes West.

In the end we walked to the exact centre of the box (confirmed by the pilot of the pick-up aircraft).

APPENDIX TWO

POLE DEFINITIONS

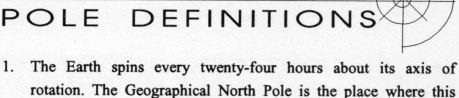

1. The Earth spins every twenty-four hours about its axis of rotation. The Geographical North Pole is the place where this axis meets the Earth's surface. Position 90°.

2. The Earth's magnetic field has both strength and direction, the latter being measured by the angles of declination and dip. The point where the field direction is directly downward to the North Magnetic Pole. Here the dip is 90° and the declination is undefined. Position 78° North 103° West.

3. A good approximation to the Earth's magnetic field is the field that would be produced by an extremely strong bar magnet placed at the Earth's centre and tilted at an angle of about 11° to the axis of rotation. The place, in the northern hemisphere, where this bar magnet, produced, meets the Earth's surface is the North Geometric Pole. Position 79.12° North 71° 12 West.

APPENDIX THREE

WIND CHILL

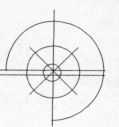

WIND SPEED			LOCAL TEMPERATURE										
M.P.H.	K.P.H.	°F	32	23	14	5	-4	-13	-22	-31	-40	-49	-58
		°C	0	-5	-10	-15	-20	-25	-30	-35	-40	-45	-50
5			29	20	10	1	-9	-18	-28	-37	-47	-56	-65
	8		-2	-7	-12	-17	-23	-28	-33	-38	-44	-49	-54
10			18	7	-4	-15	-26	-37	-48	-59	-70	-81	-92
	16		-8	-14	-20	-26	-32	-38	-44	-51	-57	-63	-69
15			13	-1	-13	-25	-37	-49	-61	-73	-85	-97	-109
	24		-11	-18	-25	-32	-38	-45	-52	-58	-65	-72	-78
20			7	-6	-19	-32	-44	-57	-70	-83	-96	-109	-121
	32		-14	-21	-28	-36	-42	-49	-57	-64	-71	-78	-85
25			3	-10	-24	-37	-50	-64	-77	-90	-104	-117	-130
	40		-16	-23	-31	-38	-46	-53	-61	-68	-76	-83	-90
30			1	-13	-27	-41	-54	-68	-82	-97	-109	-123	-137
	48		-17	-25	-33	-41	-48	-56	-63	-72	-78	-86	-94
35			-1	-15	-29	-43	-57	-71	-85	-99	-113	-127	-142
	56		-18	-26	-34	-42	-49	-57	-65	-73	-81	-88	-97
40			-3	-17	-31	-45	-59	-74	-87	-102	-116	-131	-145
	64		-19	-27	-35	-43	-51	-59	-66	-74	-82	-91	-98
45			-3	-18	-32	-46	-61	-75	-89	-104	-118	-132	-147
	72		-19	-28	-36	-43	-52	-59	-67	-75	-83	-91	-99
50			-4	-18	-33	-47	-62	-76	-91	-105	-120	-134	-148
	80		-20	-28	-36	-44	-52	-60	-68	-76	-84	-92	-100

LITTLE DANGER

CONSIDERABLE DANGER
FLESH MAY FREEZE WITHIN ONE MINUTE

VERY GREAT DANGER
FLESH MAY FREEZE WITHIN 30 SECONDS

SPONSORS

MAIN SPONSOR: ADVANTEK Inc, USA

Swiss Tourist Board

Robnorganic Systems Limited

Ciba Geigy Polymers

Raychem

3M

Shell Chemicals

Bond Publicity

Manor Press

Zannusi

John Burn Chemicals

Johnson Mathey

Musical Media

Coopers Metals

Brittania Music Club

Jaeger Clothing

Arkells Brewery

Lyons Tetley

Zermatt Tourist Board

Polycrown Limited

Donald Murray Papers

Deutch Gramaphone

Salamande

Drewette Neate

Trans XL

Sprayway Clothing

North Face

Sub Zero

Chilprufe

Whitehead Mann

Umbro Clothing

Nike Shoes

National Westminster Bank

W.L. Gore & Associates

ITN

Burton McCall Limited	BBC
A.D. Design	John Burgess Rucksacs
Central Engineering	Armstrong Products
Fischer Skis	Awards International
Berwin Bindings	Malcolm Harris Solicitors
Complete Vehicles	Thrings & Long Solicitors
Burmah Oil	Canadian Rubber
K.P.M.G. Peat Marwick	Canadian Airlines
Yuassa Batteries	Nicholas
Anchor Chemicals	Ron Hill Sports
New Chapel Electronics	Kellogs
Farepak Hampers	Walklets Partners
Harvey Sherry	Flectalon Limited
Motorola Limited	Elida Gibbs
Body Shop	Black & Decker
Cadbury's Bournville	Ambrosia
Polygram Classics	Optimus International
Koffman Footwear	Canon Cameras
Kodak Film	Matterson Walls Limited
Seiko Watches	Heinz Limited
Casio Watches	Viking Optical
Quaker Oats	Weetabix Limited
Pringles	Gates Rubber Co
Mars Limited	Premier Brands

C.P.C. (UK) Limited

Conrad Ripblat

Timberland Shoes (USA)

Thorlo Socks

Sony

Cotswold Camping

Ralston Energy Systems

British Telecom

Trimble

Photo Set

Duracell

Camping Gaz

Damart Thermolactyl

Thermarest

Atzek

DB Mountain Sport

Blacks

Tile Flair

Zippo Lighters

Argos Transmitters

Baxters Soups

HELPERS

Steve & Cathy Vincent

Georgio Matranga

Peter Hillier

Leif Lundgard

Bezal & Terry Jesudasan

Cath Whiting

Tony Harold

Chris Redman

Anita Hill

Don, Rick & Joe from Advantek

Dave Smith

Carol Karstad

Bob Meller

Bill Tidy

Peter & Leslie Broadhurst

Alan Morris

Don Hockman

Elsie Tyler

Matthew Rose

Mr & Mrs Mitchell

Mr & Mrs Saunders

Sandy Coyte

Col Andrew Croft

Ray Hally

Sue Bailey

Chris North

Martin Smith

James Lockhart

Sue Fowler

Jim Merritt

Rt Hon. John Major, MP

Rt Hon. Margaret Thatcher, MP

Reg Mann

Mary Cooney

Reese Jenkins

Dot Hudgel

Ray Shaw

Tony Slater

Len Peace	Ian Turner
Dave Schofield	Sue Harding
Darryl Oppenshaw	Emma Sage
Neil Jennings	Amanda Sage
John Allen	Peter & Sandy Praine
Ramsay James	Larry & Judy Marks
Sue Broad	Ron & Pat Brooks
Margaret Setters	Jeremy & Charlotte Brooks
Lyn Parsons	Ian & Amanda McCracken
Jackie Warwick	Mark Hempleman-Adams
Tina Stratton	Nick & Jason Hempleman
Mike Buy	Audrey Hempleman
John Mitchell	Doris Hempleman
Ian Mitchell	Jim & Eva May
Wally Herbert	Jeff May
Christine Campisano	Elaine May
Brian Bint	Shirley & Dean Chenoweth
Mike Driscoll	Thomas Sheppeard
Alex Thompson	Nick Schoon
John Knightsbridge	John Pallister
Joe Marney	John Burgess
Dick Murray	Steve Morris
Norman & Audrey Smith	Vic Sainsbury
Ray & Margaret Bibby	Mansell James

Paula Roberts

Matthew Grant

Paula Wake

Paula Lainton

Nicky Glass

Brian House

Dot Harvey

Graham Hunt

Fred Guinness

Booge

Matthew Vaughan

Simon Coombes

Eric and Eileen Rose

Jeremy Long

Alan Brickell

John Hobbs

W. Beese

Adrian Bligh

Neil McLeod

Malcolm Harris

P. Chapman

W. Newton

Judith Pickering

W. Borrell

Kadisha Buckland

Eric Owen

Ian Tubbs

Ray Dalley

Martin Tree

Alan Josling

David Whateley

Gary Farrow

John Gadd

Dr Liz Loeffler

Earnie Popkiss

Willie Hamilton

Mike Sage

Simon Davis

Alan Duckett

Mr Harrison

G. Knightly

Paul Vann

Malcolm Wallace

Kate Whiting

Mark Welsh

Karl Cleghorn

Ian Brey

M. Grey

John Hunt	Brian Moffett
G. Stamper	Alice Hamilton
Ray Beesley	M Scott
P. Austin	J. Thring
John Fiddy	Wendy Williams
Dr Hattersley-Smith	Rear Admiral R. Burn
Dale de Marchie	Maggie Coombe
Jack & Beryl Napper	Prof. David Dineley
Dr David Barraclough	Derek Laxton
Jane Harvey	Jan Caruthers
Martin Preston	John Feaver
Mrs Benady	R. Barnett
Justine Thomas	Mark Ogilvy
Gillian Smith	Philip Price
Peter Arkell	Peter Davidson
Paul Mugel	R. Hill
Susan Kelly	Liz Anderson
Sandy Sewell	J. Butter
Julian Frost	John Nelligan
Simon Taylor	Peter Knibbs
Keith Rugg	Jens Toft
Derek Waters	Nigel de Windsor
Sir John Woodward	Lord Shackleton
Dr James	Dr Robins

John Beadsmore

Ien Peace

Mr Head

David Edelston

Clive Mann

Mike Gray

Mr Peter Miller

Nick Heathcote

Clive Ferguson

Michael Jeremy

Jayne Francis

Barry Hayes

Dr Rowlands

Peter Walklets

George Pollock

A. McNally

David Smith

Sales Manager Flectalon

Charlie Campbell

Chris Cramer

Bob Meller

James Lockhart